AN INQUIRY

INTO THE

GENUINENESS OF THE MANUSCRIPT CORRECTIONS

IN

MR. J. PAYNE COLLIER'S

ANNOTATED SHAKSPERE, FOLIO, 1632;

AND OF CERTAIN SHAKSPERIAN DOCUMENTS
LIKEWISE PUBLISHED BY MR. COLLIER.

BY

N. E. S. A. HAMILTON.

LONDON:

RICHARD BENTLEY, NEW BURLINGTON STREET,

Publisher in Ordinary to Her Majesty.

MDCCCLX.

Library of Congress Cataloging in Publication Data

Hamilton, Nicholas Esterhazy Stephen Armytage, d. 1915.
   An inquiry into the genuineness of the manuscript
corrections in Mr. J. Payne Collier's annotated
Shakspere folio, 1632.

   1. Shakespeare, William, 1564-1616--Forgeries--
Collier. 2. Collier, John Payne, 1789-1883.
I. Title.
PR2951.H25 1973   822.3'3   71-168236
ISBN 0-404-03090-4

Reprinted from the edition of 1860, London
First AMS edition published in 1973
Manufactured in the United States of America

AMS PRESS INC.
NEW YORK, N.Y. 10003

AN INQUIRY

INTO THE

GENUINENESS OF THE MANUSCRIPT CORRECTIONS

IN

MR. J. PAYNE COLLIER'S

ANNOTATED SHAKSPERE, FOLIO, 1632;

AMS PRESS
NEW YORK

FACSIMILES.

PREFACE.

THE following pages are meant to redeem the pledge given to the public in *The Times* of July 2, 1859, in which a more complete examination was promised into the genuineness of numerous modern alterations in Shakspere's text, than was possible in the columns of a newspaper. The matter, I believe, has a great importance, greater than is even suspected as yet. It is really this—whether we shall retain our National Poet's works in a form approaching perfection, or miserably corrupted.

The last century saw Shakspere's text pretty nearly established. Malone, Steevens, and others, succeeded in presenting it, if not in complete purity, still as accurately as it was read by men who knew Shakspere, lived with, and survived him. The "old folios" and quartos had yielded up their readings, and the doubtful province of conjectural emendation alone remained for the most ambitious editor.

But the year 1849 saw a great change. The entirely new element of *manuscript authority* was introduced ; and under cover of this, alterations innumerable were made in the text of the Poet. If these corrections rested on a valid basis, a more signal benefit to literature had seldom been conferred; but if doubtful or spurious, then the wrong done to the cause of letters was at least as great.

The greatness and glory, however, of the discovery were well kept before the public. The few competent Shaksperian critics who dissented and raised doubts, were put to silence as frivolous or envious, and the "Old Corrector" seemed destined to become one of those

> " dead but sceptred sovereigns, who still rule
> Our spirits from their urns."

Unfortunately, those who impugned the genuineness of these alterations did so on grounds which, however scholar-like, could hardly be conclusive; whether, for instance, such and such words were in use, or bore a certain signification,

in Shakspere's time ; while others, again, con-
tented themselves with urging the improbability
of the corrections having been copied from the
prompt-books, or in exposing the absurdity
involved in the idea of a man's taking a folio to
the pit of a theatre, and correcting it on his
knee. Such criticism, while it might raise doubts,
could never turn them into certainties against
the corrections. That question could only be
settled by the genuineness or otherwise of the
corrections themselves. Were they really of the
middle of the seventeenth century, or were they
skilful imitations of a *much more recent* date?
And this could only be ascertained by a critical
examination of the handwriting of the annotations,
conducted by those well used to such inquiries.

It needs not be said that no examination of the
kind was undertaken until quite recently. The
"annotated folio," it is true, was *seen* a few times
in public, that is to say, thrice at the evening
meetings of the Society of Antiquaries, and once at
a meeting of the Shakspere Society ;* but, wonder-

---

* See Mr. Collier's Affidavit, p. 15. As early as 1853 Mr. Charles
Knight pointed out, in a temperate but forcible manner, the pro-
priety of having the " Folio " " deposited in the custody of some

ful as it may seem, notwithstanding the fierceness of controversy to which they gave rise, no one appears to have thought of submitting the marginal corrections to a strict palæographic examination, or of postponing the discussion of their *intrinsic merits* to the more important and preliminary inquiry as to the *genuineness* of their character. The book shortly passed into the hands of a late noble duke, the controversy lost the interest of novelty, and the general impression of the public, both at home and abroad, seemed to be that something very wonderful, after all, had been made out, and that Shakspere, as well as everything else now-a-days, had been "improved."

And not only Shakspere. The latter half at least of the present volume is devoted to the discussion of the genuineness of certain "documents," bearing more or less on the history of the Poet and the literature of his day. The importance of these documents is even greater than that of the "corrections." They profess to be originals; and both from the facts they contain themselves, and the

<hr />

public body, who will allow access, under proper regulations, for a full and free inspection of its contents."—*Old Lamps or New*, p. lix. Pity it is that such a course was not adopted.

light they throw on others, would be invaluable,
if authentic. Unfortunately, their importance is
much diminished by their undoubtedly spurious
nature. While it is grievous to see lessened the
scanty number of facts referring to Shakspere's
external history, that very circumstance, that we
know so little about him, renders it the more in-
cumbent upon us to be rigorous and accurate in
what we do accept concerning him. The manuscripts and papers I refer to are fully described
further on. The authenticity of several of them
has never even been questioned till now. They
have gradually filtered into our literature, and are
the cause of an ever-spreading dissemination of
error. That this should be arrested, however painful the discovery or process may prove, I think
must be desired by every friend to Letters.

This, therefore, is the ground that I take up. I
do not meddle with the *intrinsic* and purely literary
part of the question at all. I do not discuss the
date or the use of certain words. I merely examine,
on *external* grounds, the authenticity of the handwriting. While this method is a great deal more
conclusive, it is the first time it has been applied

in this discussion. If the following pages be found *dry* and technical, it is inevitable from the very nature of the inquiry. As a sense of its importance kept me up, I hope and believe a similar feeling will animate my reader. It certainly *is* no trifling matter, whether the works of one of the greatest minds that ever adorned humanity be correct or corrupt—entire or mutilated: it *is not* unimportant that in our time, and before our eyes, we should see their grandeur defaced and their purity stained. And not easily forgiven should we be, if, seeing this, we strove not to hinder it.

It merely remains to add, that throughout this self-imposed task, the notion of a personal controversy or dispute has never guided my pen. This disclaimer, while it is superfluous for my friends, I wish pointedly directed to the notice of the public. My aim has been to remove from English literature a discreditable imposition. If one or more are aggrieved by the results I have come to, I regret but cannot help it. While I ask for no favour, I can show no partiality. My inquiries have no recommendation but their honesty and candour; and if they receive from competent judges the verdict of Truth, I shall be amply rewarded, and feel that my labour has not been in vain.

Before concluding this prefatory statement, I have one duty left which fills me with unmixed pleasure—the offer of my grateful thanks to those to whom I am indebted for the opportunity of bringing this Inquiry before the public, or who have assisted me with their aid and counsel in a labour of no slight difficulty and of grave responsibility.

To his Grace the Duke of Devonshire, for the courtesy with which he placed the volume under discussion at my disposal, and permitted me not only to publish fac-similes of the pen and pencil corrections on its margins, but also to make several important physical experiments in regard to them.

To the Right Hon. the Earl of Ellesmere, for the liberality with which he gave me access to his Library, and permitted me to make use of his unique copy of the first folio edition of Shakspere's Plays, as well as to examine and have fac-similes taken of the disputed Shakspere documents at Bridgewater House.

To the Governors of Dulwich College, for the
ready access I obtained to their valuable muni-
ments; and especially to the Rev. Alfred Carver,
the Master of the College, for the friendly aid
which converted what might possibly be esteemed
an ordinary civility paid to literary men, into a
lasting personal obligation to myself.

To my friends and colleagues in the British
Museum, whom I gladly avail myself of the opportunity of thanking for the unvarying kindness
I have ever received from them in my literary pur-
suits. Above all to Sir Frederic Madden, the chief
of the Department to which I have the honour to
belong, and to whom an acknowledgment is due,
beyond the mere expression of my thanks for the
invaluable assistance of his observations and
experience. It is, indeed, a simple act of honesty
and justice alike to him and to the world, that I
should state the origin of the discovery presumed
to be established in the following pages. The
'Annotated Shakspere' was placed in Sir F.
Madden's hands by the Duke of Devonshire.
His independent examination of it completely
convinced him of the fictitious character of the

writing of the marginal corrections; and this conclusion he freely communicated to inquirers interested in knowing it. The correspondence between certain pencil-marks in the margins with corrections in ink, first noticed by myself, led him to a closer examination of the volume, and to the detection of numerous marks of punctuation and entire words in pencil, and in a modern character, in connection with the pretended older writing in ink; instances of which were subsequently found to occur on nearly every page. It was, moreover, owing in a great measure to Sir Frederic Madden's encouragement that I was originally induced to bestow that attention to the subject, which has developed the inquiry to its present results.

To the numerous other friends who have aided and assisted me in my labour, I have to tender the general expression of a gratitude as lively as it is sincere.

N. E. S. A. HAMILTON.

Department of Manuscripts, British Museum,
January, 1860.

AN INQUIRY, ETC.

In the year 1852, Mr. John Payne Collier published a volume of " *Notes and Emendations* " of the Plays of Shakspere, derived from a corrected copy of the second edition, in folio, 1632, the history of which he gives in the Introduction to the volume, as follows :—

" In the spring of 1849 I happened to be in the shop of the late Mr. Rodd, of Great Newport Street, at the time when a package of books arrived from the country ; my impression is that it came from Bedfordshire, but I am not at all certain upon a point which I looked upon as a matter of no importance. He opened the parcel in my presence, as he had often done before in the course of my thirty or forty years' acquaintance with him, and looking at the backs and title-pages of several volumes, I saw that they were chiefly works of little interest to me. Two folios, however, attracted my attention, one of them gilt on the sides, and the other in rough calf :

the first was an excellent copy of Florio's "New World of Words," 1611, with the name of Henry Osborn (whom I mistook at the moment for his celebrated namesake, Francis) upon the first leaf; and the other a copy of the second folio of Shakespeare's Plays, much cropped, the covers old and greasy, and, as I saw at a glance on opening them, imperfect at the beginning and end.   Concluding hastily that the latter would complete another poor copy of the second folio, which I had bought of the same bookseller, and which I had had for some years in my possession, and wanting the former for my use, I bought them both,—the Florio for twelve, and the Shakespeare for thirty shillings.*

"As it turned out, I at first repented my bargain as regarded the Shakespeare, because when I took it home it appeared that two leaves which I wanted were unfit

---

* "I paid the money for them at the time. Mr. Wilkinson, of Wellington Street, one of Mr. Rodd's executors, has several times obligingly afforded me the opportunity of inspecting Mr. Rodd's account-books, in order, if possible, to trace from whence the package came, but without success. Mr. Rodd does not appear to have kept any stock-book, showing how and when volumes came into his hands, and the entries in his day-book and ledger are not regular nor particular. His latest memorandum, on 19th April, only a short time before his sudden death, records the sale of "three books," without specifying their titles, or giving the name of the purchaser. His memory was very faithful, and to that, doubtless, he often trusted. I am confident that the parcel was from the country; but any inquiries regarding sales there, could hardly be expected to be satisfactorily answered."—[C.]

for my purpose, not merely by being too short, but damaged and defaced : thus disappointed, I threw it by, and did not see it again until I made a selection of books I would take with me on quitting London. In the mean time, finding that I could not readily remedy the deficiencies in my other copy of the folio 1632, I had parted with it ; and when I removed into the country with my family, in the spring of 1850, in order that I might not be without some copy of the second folio, for the purpose of reference, I took with me that which is the foundation of the present work.

"It was while putting my books together for removal that I first observed some marks in the margin of this folio ; but it was subsequently placed upon an upper shelf, and I did not take it down until I had occasion to consult it. It then struck me that Thomas Perkins, whose name, with the addition of "his Booke," was upon the cover, might be the old actor who had performed in Marlowe's "Jew of Malta," on its revival shortly before 1633. At this time I fancied that the binding was of about that date, and that the volume might have been his ; but in the first place I found that his name was Richard Perkins, and in the next I became satisfied that the rough calf was not the original binding. Still, Thomas Perkins might have been a descendant of Richard ; and this circumstance, and others, induced me to examine the volume more particularly. I then discovered, to my surprise, that there was hardly a page which did not present, in a handwriting of the time, some emendation in the pointing or in the text, while on most of them they were frequent, and on many numerous.

" Of course I now submitted the folio to a most careful scrutiny ; and as it occupied a considerable time to complete the inspection, how much more must it have consumed to make the alterations ? The ink was of various shades, differing sometimes on the same page, and I was once disposed to think that two distinct hands had been employed upon them : this notion I have since abandoned ; and I am now decidedly of opinion that the same writing prevails from beginning to end, but that the amendments must have been introduced from time to time, during perhaps the course of several years. The changes in punctuation alone, always made with nicety and patience, must have required a long period, considering their number : the other alterations, sometimes most minute, extending even to turned letters, and typographical trifles of that kind, from their very nature, could not have been introduced with rapidity, while many of the errata must have severely tasked the industry of the old corrector."*

* " It ought to be mentioned, in reference to the question of the authority of the emendations, that some of them are upon erasures, as if the corrector had either altered his mind as to particular changes, or had obliterated something that had been written before—possibly by some person not so well informed as himself."—[C.] I may remark, in reference to this note by Mr. Collier, that the erasures and obliterations are very numerous, and both they and the corrections *are by one and the same hand throughout the volume*. Of those partially obliterated I have given some examples in the collations from Hamlet.—[H.]

The veracity of this account Mr. Collier reiterated in an Affidavit sworn to in the Court of Queen's Bench in 1856.

" AFFIDAVIT.

" IN THE QUEEN'S BENCH.

" I, John Payne Collier, of Maidenhead, in the County of Berks, Esquire, Barrister-at-Law, and one of the Vice-Presidents of the Society of Antiquaries of London, make oath and say :—

" 1. That in the years 1841, 1842, 1843, and 1844, I prepared for the press, and published an edition of the works of Shakespeare : that in the spring of the year 1849 I purchased of the late Mr. Rodd, of Great Newport Street, bookseller, a copy of the second folio of Shakespeare's Plays, bearing the date of, and which I believe was published in the year 1632 ; and which copy contained, when I so purchased it, a great number of manuscript notes, purporting to be corrections, alterations, and emendations of the original text, made, as I believe, by the same person, and at a period nearly contemporaneous with the publication of the said folio itself.

" 2. In order that any person interested in the subject might have an opportunity of inspecting the said book, and examining the said manuscript notes, I exhibited the said book to and before the Shakespeare Society, and three times before the Society of Antiquaries, and it was inspected and examined by a great number of persons. The said folio has, since the publication of the volume next hereinafter mentioned, become, and is now, the property of his Grace the Duke of Devonshire.

" 3. In the year 1852 I published a volume containing some, but not all, of the said manuscript corrections, alterations, and emendations, and a fac-simile of a part of one page of the said folio, with the manuscript emendations thereon ; and an 'Introduction,' setting forth the circumstances under which I became possessed of the said folio edition, and which induced me to publish the said volume.

" 4. In the year 1853 I published a second edition of the said Notes and Emendations, containing, besides the said 'Introduction,' a statement, in the form of a Preface to the last-mentioned edition, of facts and circumstances which occurred subsequently to the publication of my first edition of the said 'Notes and Emendations '— a copy of which second edition is now shown to me and marked with the letter A. And I say, that all the statements in the said Preface and Introduction, relative to the discovery, contents, and authenticity of the said folio copy, and the manuscript notes, corrections, alterations, and emendations thereof are true ; and that every note, correction, alteration, and emendation in each of the said two editions, and every word, figure, and sign therein, purporting or professing to be a note, correction, alteration, or emendation of the text, is, to the best of my knowledge and belief, a true and accurate copy of the original manuscript in the said folio copy of 1632; and that I have not, in either of the said editions, to the best of my knowledge and belief, inserted a single

word, stop, sign, note, correction, alteration, or emendation of the said original text of Shakespeare, which is not
a faithful copy of the said original manuscript,* and which
I do not believe to have been written, as aforesaid, not
long after the publication of the said folio copy of the
year 1632," &c. [The remainder of the affidavit refers
to the *Coleridge Lectures,* published by Mr. Collier in
1856.—H.]

"(Signed) JOHN PAYNE COLLIER."

"Sworn at the Judge's Chambers,
    Rolls Garden, Chancery Lane,
    this 8th day of January, 1856,
    before me, Wm. Clark, Com-
    missioner, &c."

---

* Apparently Mr. Collier has since altered his opinion as to
the respect due to the "said original manuscript," to the extent
of occasionally *correcting the Corrector.* Of this, I quote the following singular instance from the play of Coriolanus. In his
first edition of the MS. corrections, Mr. Collier announced the
important and truly interesting fact, that in Act iii. sc. 2, of
that drama a whole line had been left out in all preceding editions, and was now restored through the help and accuracy of
the invaluable Corrector. Here is the passage—Volumnia
says :—

> "Pray be counsailed,
> I have a heart as little apt as yours
> *To brook control without the use of anger,*
> But yet a braine, that leads my use of anger
> To better vantage."

The third line in italics being the new discovery ; and it remained as above accurately copied from the corrected folio for
six years, viz. in the *Notes and Emendations,* 1852 and 1853, in

D

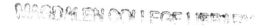

On the 2nd and 16th of July, 1859, I laid
before the public, through the medium of *The
Times*, a summary of facts to prove that the *Notes*

---

the privately distributed fac-similes, in the one-volume Shakspere, and in the Complete List, 1856.

Strange as it may seem, in the last edition, of 1858, Mr. Collier
has substituted "reproof" instead of "control" *as the emendation of the "Old Corrector,"* and this, notwithstanding the scru-
pulous accuracy with which he would lead us to suppose he
invariably followed his venerable and *manuscript* authority.

I contrast Mr. Collier's first version of the line printed in
Notes and Emendations, 1852, with his account of it in his last
edition of Shakspere's Works, 1858.

Notes and Emendations, Coriolanus, Act iii. sc. 2, J. P.
Collier, 1852.

"(P. 212) On the same evidence, we here recover a line,
which is certainly wanting in the old copies, since they leave
the sense incomplete without it. It is in Volumnia's entreaty
to her son —

> "Pray be counsell'd.
> I have a heart as little apt as yours,
> But yet a brain, that leads my use of anger
> To better vantage."

"To what was Volumnia's heart 'as little apt' as that of
Coriolanus? The insertion of a missing line (the absence of
which has not hitherto been suspected) enables us to give the
answer :—

> "I have a heart as little apt as yours
> *To brook control without the use of anger,*
> But yet a brain, that leads my use of anger
> To better vantage."

"The line in italics is written in a blank space, and a mark
made to where it ought to come in. The compositor was,

and Emendations contained in Mr. Collier's annotated copy of Shakspere's Plays, 1632, were
in reality modern fabrications of our own day,
although written in a feigned hand intended to
represent the style of writing common in the
seventeenth century; and that the statement of
Mr. Collier that the volume, "from the first page
to the last, contained notes and emendations in a
handwriting *not much later* than the time when
it came from the press," was incorrect.

Several months have elapsed since these facts
were published, but no satisfactory attempt has
been made by Mr. Collier to refute them, or to

---

doubtless, misled by the recurrence of the same words at the
ends of the two lines, and carelessly omitted the first. From
whence, if not from some independent authority, whether heard
or read, was this addition to the text derived?"

Shakespeare's Works, ed. Collier, 1858.—Coriolanus, Act iii. sc. 2.

> " Pray be counsell'd.
>
> I have a heart as little apt as yours
> To brook reproof without the use of anger,[1]
> But yet a brain," &c.
>
> [1] (" TO BROOK REPROOF WITHOUT THE USE OF ANGER.")

"This line is from the corr. fo. 1632, and is clearly wanted,
since the sense is incomplete without it. The eye of the old
compositor was doubtless misled by the words 'use of anger' at
the end of two following lines. Those who are unwilling to
insert the line are obliged to suppose Volumnia to speak ellip-
tically; but until the discovery of the corr. fo. 1632, nobody suspected even an ellipsis. We rejoice in the discovery."

remove the stigma of forgery from his " folio."
I must therefore suppose that he is aware of
the impossibility of doing this, and that he is
now at length convinced of the spurious character
of the corrections ; the more so as he has proffered
no explanation of the circumstances by which he
may have been himself originally deceived, or of
the reasons which induced him to accept and publish as genuine emendations of the seventeenth
century, what in fact it requires no rigorous
examination to discover are worthless counterfeits
of the nineteenth.

As in denouncing the character of the corrections, the only objects I had in view were the
vindication of truth, and the desire to warn the
world of the spurious nature of the " emendations "
by which they had been too readily deceived,
I would gladly have left the more minute features
of the case to be developed by the recognised
guardians of Shaksperian literature.   Above all,
I naturally supposed that Mr. Collier (who alone
has introduced into his editions of Shakspere the
corrections derived from this Folio, and to whom
the discovery of the Folio itself is due,) would have
hastened to lend his aid to sift to the bottom the
particular evidences against the credibility of the
volume, which I had brought so distinctly and

prominently to his notice. In this, however, I was mistaken. So far from assisting in an inquiry, in the results of which he, more than any living man, must have been deeply interested, he has only broken silence to give utterance to a desire, rather petulantly expressed, and under the circumstances impossible to regard, that he and his Folio might be let alone, and considered privileged from further scrutiny.

I may have regretted this expression of feeling on Mr. Collier's part as an error of judgment; but I feel less concern in regard to the line of conduct adopted by some other and later champions of the Folio, who, in their need of argument forgetting the duty of courtesy, seem to have imagined that the civilities of ordinary life do not extend to literary disputants. However, on all sides, "fuller and further particulars" were called for; and as, in the course of my inquiries, I had made the extraordinary discovery that not only in reference to the corrected folio of 1632, but in other instances in which Mr. Collier had published "facts" and "documents," relative to Shakspere, these facts and documents turned out on investigation to be likewise spurious, I have resolved to lay before the world all the results of my investigations, leaving any inferences deducible from them to the judgment of the individual reader.

On the 18th of May, 1859, Sir Frederic Madden, Keeper of the MSS. in the British Museum, attaching at that time, as I understand,* no great importance to the various doubts respecting the authenticity of the corrections in the annotated folio 1632, which from time to time had reached him, but having a great desire to inspect the volume for his own information, wrote to the Duke of Devonshire begging the loan of it for a short time, for the satisfaction of himself, Dr. Bodenstedt of Munich, and a few friends.

On the 26th, the book was placed in Sir Frederic's hands, and, at his request, a discretionary power was shortly after granted him by the noble owner, to exhibit the book to a more

---

* In a memorandum communicated to me by Sir Frederic Madden, he states—" I had a great wish to see the volume, after this second avowal of doubts expressed by Mr. Staunton and Dr. Ingleby, but my mind was so free from any bias, that I did not entertain the least suspicion of forgery, and in September, 1858, I eagerly availed myself of the opportunity afforded me by Mr. Collier (who had sent me a copy of the Hamlet of 1603, lithographed at the expense of the late Duke of Devonshire), to express to him *my wish to see the annotated folio*, but not having the honour to be acquainted with the now Duke of Devonshire, I asked Mr. Collier *if he could manage to gain me access to the volume*. To this request Mr. Collier never made any reply."

extended literary circle, in consequence of the numerous applications to see it, which had been sent in, as soon as it was known to be at the Museum. In accordance with this permission, a considerable number of persons interested in the matter did so examine the volume during the period it remained in the Museum, and no application to see it was declined, except during the brief period in which Mr. Frederick Netherclift was occupied in making from it the fac-similes pre-fixed to this volume.

Such were the circumstances under which the "Folio" came into the Museum; and it was not at first imagined that anything would result from its examination tending to invalidate the manuscript corrections on its margins.

A short inspection, however, of the ink corrections in the text and on the margins was sufficient to give rise to the gravest doubts as to their genuineness. In the first place, although evidently written by one hand throughout, yet the forms of the letters, especially of the capital letters, presented strange anomalies. On one page would be found a word or letter, characteristic rather of the writing of the 16th than of the 17th century; while in close juxtaposition, and some-times on the same page, the identical letter or

word would occur, bearing every appearance of
having been written within the present century.

Then, again, many of the letters, although executed with evident care, were seen to be rather
exaggerations of the style of the 17th century
than examples of the style itself; while instances
occur in almost every page, in which the operator,
apparently not satisfied with his first attempt at an
antique appearance, has subsequently retouched
his work, in a manner greatly calculated to arouse
suspicion, as the ink employed for the purpose is not
uncommonly of a different shade, and the stroke of
a different thickness from that in which the word
or letter was originally written.   Thus, on mere
palæographic grounds, the authenticity of the
corrections appeared questionable.   But it was
further discovered, and this, too, before the whole
weight of these *literal* objections had been fully
considered, that a series of partially-obliterated
pencil corrections was visible throughout the
margins of the Folio, *corresponding* with the corrections made in ink, and sometimes *actually
underlying* them.   The appearances presented by
these pencil corrections merit exact description.

In the first place, they have none of the feigned
antiquity about them of the ink corrections, either
in form or spelling.   They are in a bold, clear

handwriting of the present day, are evidently executed by one hand throughout, and have been placed
on the margins to direct the alterations afterwards
made in ink, and with which they invariably corre-
spond. They are of various kinds. Amongst the
most common are crosses and ticks, apparently
used to call attention to words or letters requiring
correction. Some of them may, of course, be the
"crosses, ticks, or lines" which Mr. Collier acknow-
ledges he introduced himself; but as cases occur
where such pencil-ticks actually *underlie* corrections in ink, some of them at least must have been
placed on the margins before the "Old Corrector"
commenced his labours. The ordinary signs in
use to indicate *corrigenda* for the press are of
common occurrence in the margins, while the
corrections indicated thereby are made in the text
in the *quasi*-antique ink. Again, whole syllables
or words occur in pencil, partially rubbed out,
but still legible, and in which the character of the
modern handwriting is plainly visible; while in
near neighbourhood to them, the same syllable or
word is repeated in ink in the antique hand. In
some cases the ink word and the pencil word
occupy the same space in the margin, and are
written one upon the other; and in these instances
the naked eye readily detects the fact that the

E

pencil has been written prior to the ink. As, however, the most positive evidence on this head was desirable, its decision forming one of the turning-points of the inquiry, Mr. Maskelyne, by permission of the Duke of Devonshire, undertook to institute a series of microscopic and chemical experiments on the subject. The importance of the point lay in this : that since the pencil alterations were undeniably recent (as a glance at the fac-similes prefixed to this volume will show), it followed that the ink corrections, if written subsequently to these, must be modern likewise, however carefully an antique appearance might have been simulated for them. Mr. Maskelyne's experiments set this point completely at rest, and at the same time elicited several particulars as to the chemical composition and spurious character of the ink itself. It was, in fact, proved by scientific demonstration, that the antique-looking alterations in ink were not so venerable as the modern pencilling ; that they were in reality modern fabrications, although executed with such dexterity as to deceive on a cursory glance even an experienced eye. So important are these experiments, that I re-state them here in Mr. Maskelyne's own words.   He says :—

" This simple test (the microscope) of the character of

these emendations, I brought to bear on them, and with the following results :—

" Firstly, as to any question that might be raised concerning the presence of the pencil-marks asserted to be so plentifully distributed down the margin, the answer is, they are there. The microscope reveals the particles of plumbago in the hollows of the paper, and in no case that I have yet examined does it fail to bring this fact forward into incontrovertible reality. Secondly, the ink presents a rather singular aspect under the microscope. Its appearance in many cases on, rather than in, the paper, suggested the idea of its being a water-colour paint rather than an ink ; it has a remarkable lustre, and the distribution of particles of colouring matter in it seems unlike that in inks, ancient or modern, that I have yet examined.

" This view is somewhat confirmed by a taste, unlike the styptic taste of ordinary inks, which it imparts to the tongue, and by its substance evidently yielding to the action of damp. But on this point, as on another, to which attention will presently be drawn, it was not possible to arrive at a satisfactory conclusion in the absence of the Duke of Devonshire's permission to make a few experiments on the volume.

" His Grace visited the Museum yesterday, and was good enough to give me his consent to this. The result has been that the suspicions previously entertained regarding the ink were confirmed.

" It proves to be a paint removable, with the exception of a slight stain, by mere water, while, on the other hand, its colouring matter resists the action of chymical agents which rapidly change inks, ancient or modern, whose colour is due to iron. In some places, indeed, this paint seems to have become mixed, accidentally or otherwise, with ordinary ink, but its prevailing character is that of a paint formed perhaps of sepia, or of sepia mixed with a little Indian ink. This, however, is of secondary importance in comparison with the other point which has been alluded to. This point involves, indeed, the most important question that has arisen, and concerns the relative dates of the modern-looking pencil-marks and the old emendations of the text which are in ink. The pencil-marks are of different kinds. Some are *d's*, indicative of the deletion of stops or letters in the text, and to which alterations in ink, I believe, invariably respond. Others, again, belong to the various modes at present in use to indicate corrigenda for the press. Some may, perhaps, be the " crosses, ticks, or lines," which Mr. Collier introduced himself. But there are others again in which whole syllables or words in pencil are not so effectually rubbed out as not to be still traceable and legible, and even the character of the handwriting discernible, while in near neighbourhood to them the same syllable or word is repeated in the paint-like ink before described. The pencil is in a modern-looking hand, the ink in a quaint antique-looking writing. In several cases, however, the ink word and the pencil word occupy the same ground in the margin, and are one over the other. The question that arises in these cases, of whether these two

writings are both ancient or both modern, or one ancient and the other modern, is a question for the antiquary or palæographist. The question of whether the
pencil is antecedent or subsequent to the ink is resolvable into a physical inquiry as to whether the ink overlies the pencil, or the pencil is superposed upon the ink.
The answer to this question is as follows :—

" I have nowhere been able to detect the pencil-marks
clearly overlying the ink, though in several places the
pencil stops abruptly at the ink, and in some seems to
be just traceable through its translucent substance,
while lacking there the generally metallic lustre of the
plumbago. But the question is set at rest by the removal by water of the ink in instances where the ink
and the pencil intersected each other. The first case I
chose for this was a *u* in *Richard II.*, p. 36. A pencil
tick crossed the *u*, intersecting each limb of that letter.
The pencil was barely visible through the first stroke,
and not at all visible under the second stroke of the *u*.
On damping off the ink in the first stroke, however, the
pencil-mark became much plainer than before, and even
when as much of the inkstain as possible was removed,
the pencil still runs through the ink line in unbroken
even continuity. Had the pencil been superposed on
the ink, it must have lain superficially upon its lustrous
surface, and have been removed in the washing. We
must, I think, be led by this to the inference that the
pencil underlies the ink—that is to say, was antecedent
to it in its date ; while, also, it is evident that the " old
commentator " had done his best to rub out the pencil

writing before he introduced its ink substitute."—*Times*, *July* 16, 1859.

It seemed incomprehensible how these various and irrefragable proofs of forgery could have escaped Mr. Collier, considering the "most careful scrutiny" to which he states he committed the folio. But I now began to compare the marginal corrections with Mr. Collier's Complete List of them, published in 1856, and with very singular results. The *List* professes to give, in a tabular form, the "entire body" of the emendations. Nothing can be more clear than this. It is not only indicated by the title,* but asserted in the strongest manner in the preface, as the following extracts show. Mr. Collier says :—

"These *Notes and Emendations* are before the world in two separate editions; but as the whole of the alterations and corrections were not included, and as those interested in such matters are anxious to see *the entire body* in the shortest form, I have appended them to the present volume in one column, while in the opposite column I have placed the old, or the received text. Thus a comparison may be made in an instant, as to the

---

* "A List of *every* MS. Note and Emendation in Mr. Collier's copy of Shakespeare's Works, folio, 1632." (Appended to Coleridge's "Lectures on Shakespeare and Milton," ed. J. P. Collier. London, 1856. Octavo.)

particular letters, syllables, words, or lines in which changes have been introduced."—*Preface to Coleridge's Seven Lectures*, p. 60.

Again, Mr. Collier says :—

" I have gone over *every* emendation in the folio 1632, recently, for the purpose of the last portion of my present volume ; and I am more and more convinced, that the great majority of the corrections were made, not from better manuscripts, still less from unknown printed copies of the plays, but from the recitation of old actors while the performance was proceeding."—*Preface to Seven Lectures*, p. 73.

And still further he adds :—

" Fault has been found with me, in other quarters, for not having at once seen everything in the way of MS. note in my folio 1632. I have often gone over the thousands of marks of all kinds in its margins ; but I will take this opportunity of pointing out two emendations of considerable importance, which, happening not to be in the margins, and being written with very pale ink, escaped my eye until some time after the appearance of my second edition, as well as of the one-volume Shakespeare. For the purpose of the later portion of my present work *I have recently re-examined every line and letter of the folio 1632, and I can safely assert that no other sin of omission on my part can be discovered.*"—*Preface to Seven Lectures*, p. 79.

And yet in spite of these reiterated assertions,

the *literal* fact is, that the Complete List does
not contain one *half* of the corrections, many of
the most significant being among those omitted.
That it may be seen this is no exaggerated statement, I subjoin a collation of the entire play
of *Hamlet*; the collations faithfully representing
the "emendations on the margins of the folio."
Such of them as Mr. Collier has inserted in his
Complete List being indicated by a capital C.   I
have likewise, through the kind assistance of my
friend Mr. Howard Staunton, indicated the original sources, from which the principal corrections
have been derived.   Many of my readers will
probably be surprised to see the number of them
which can be thus identified, and the small claims
to originality which the " Old Corrector " actually
possesses.   Some of the readings not given in the
List are certainly to be met with in the one-
volume edition of Shakspere, published by Mr.
Collier in 1853; but the text of that volume,
although purporting to be "regulated by the
recently discovered folio of 1632," sometimes
follows the printed folios of the first and second
edition, sometimes the MS. corrections in the
folio 1632, and sometimes the quartos, and is
therefore, as a book of reference, utterly worthless, it being impossible for the reader to dis-

criminate from what source any given reading is derived. "The truth is," says a sound Shaksperian critic (Grant White), "that the text of the pernicious one-volume edition, professing to be 'regulated by the recently discovered folio of 1632, containing early MS. emendations,' is composed from the readings of the first folio, the uncorrected second folio, Mr. Collier's corrected second folio, and all other previous and subsequent editions; the changes from the first folio, or from any other edition, being in no way indicated. To the well-read, critical student of the text, the book is useless; to him who has but commenced his studies, indescribably confusing; to the general reader, a delusion and a snare. With all respect due from me to a gentleman who was a man when my father was a boy, I must say that the publication of that volume was a crime against the republic of letters."

"EMENDATIONS" IN THE PLAY OF "HAMLET," FROM THE "CORRECTED FOLIO" 1632.

[The left-hand column contains the printed text of the folio 1632. The words, letters, &c., to the right placed between crotchets, refer to words, letters, &c. in italic, and placed between crotchets in the text, and exhibit the manuscript "*corrections*" found on the margins of Mr. J. P. Collier's "Corrected Folio," 1632, such of these as have been published by Mr. Collier in the Complete List being distinguished by the letter C. The foot-notes show the sources from which the manuscript corrections to which they refer were originally derived.]

	Printed Text of Folio 1632.	*MS. Corrections.*
p. 272, col. 1.	ʌ	[Act I.]
	Enter BERNARDO *and* FRANCISCO.	
	BAR. Tis n[o]w struck twelve[,] get thee to bed ʌ Francisco.	[e][1] C.[:] [,]
	[MAR.] What, ha's this thing appear'd againe	[HOR.][2]
	Wh[o]n yond same Starre ʌ thats Westward	[e][3] [,]
col. 2.	The Bell then [beating] one	[tolling] this in a modern hand in ink, but afterwards partially obliterated.
	Enter the Ghost ʌ.	[armed]
	BAR. Looke ʌ it not like the King?	[s][4]
	HOR. Most like [:]	[.] with pencil cross in margin.
	When ʌ th' Ambitious Norway combatted	[he][5] C.
	He smot ʌ the sledded Pollax	[e] with pencil mark.
	MAR. Thus twice before, and just at this [same] houre	[dead][6] afterwards part. oblit.
	HOR. In what particular [thoughte to] worke	[it] partially obliterated.

[1] Steevens. [2] 4to 1604. [3] 4tos and fol. 1623. [4] 4tos. [5] 4tos. [6] Fol. 1623, and 1st and 2nd 4tos.

Printed Text of Folio 1632.	*MS. Corrections.*
MAR. Good now͵ sit downe, and tell me͵ he that knowes͵	[, , ,] with pencil mark.
Do's not divide the Sunday from the weeke[,]	[?]¹ with pencil mark.
p. 273, Which he stood seiz'd [*o*]n,	[1]
col. 1. Was gaged by our King : which had re[*turn'd*]	[maind] partially obliterated.
And carriage of the Article [*de*]sign'd	[then ?] afterwards oblit.
Shark'd up a List of L[*and*]lesse Resolutes	[aw]² C.

͵ Enter Ghost againe.

	Entire line of Stage direction obliterated.
Which happily foreknow[*ing*] may avoyd	[ledge] partially obliterated.
Speake of it. Stay, and speake. Stop it, Marcellus.	[*Cock crowes*]³
The Cocke that is the Trumpet to the [*day*]	[morne]⁴ C.
Some saye[*s*], that ever 'gainst that season	crossed out.
And͵ (they say) no spirit can walke abroad	[then]⁵
No Faiery ta[*l*]kes	crossed out. C.
p. 273,[But looke, the Morne in Russet Mantle clad,	These two lines crossed through.
col. 2. Walkes o're the Dew of yon high Easterne hill.]	A pencil × in margin.

OPHELIA, Lords Attendants. ͵

To [*beare*] our hearts in griefe	[*King takes his seate*]
⌈With one Auspicious, and one Dropping eye,	[bathe] C.
With mirth in Funerall, & with Dirge in Marriage,	
In equall Scale weighing Delight and Dole]	These lines crossed out.
Colleagued with the dreame of ͵his Advantage [;]	[t] partially obliterated. [,]
Of these dilated Articles allow [:]͵	[.] [Give them]
p. 274, ⌈beg Laertes	
col. 1. *to*	Crossed out.
What wouldst thou have Laertes?]	

---

¹ Jennens.   ² 4tos.   ³ 4to 1604   ⁴ 4to 1605.   ⁵ 4tos & folio 1623.

Printed Text of Folio 1632.	MS. Corrections.

HAM. A little more then kin, and lesse then kind. [(*Aside*)][1]

QUEE. Good Hamlet cast thy nightl [*y*] colour off [ike] C.

Doe not for ever, with thy v[*e*]yled lids [a][2]

[It shewes a will most incorrect to Heaven

          to   Crossed out.

As any the most vulgar thing to sence.]

    [————— Fye, tis a fault to heaven

          to   Crossed out.

This must be so.]

p. 274,
col. 2. And the King's Rou[*c*]e[,] the heavens, &c. [s][3] [dele]

        Manet HAMLET. [*Trumpets*]

Seeme[*s*] to me all the uses of this world [dele][4]

Fye on't? Oh fie, [*fie,*] tis an unweeded Garden [dele][5]

That he might not [*beteene*] the windes of heaven [let e'en][6] but afterwards
                                          partially obliterated.

Visit her face too roughly. Heaven and Earth[,] [!][7]

Must I remember[:] why. she would hang on him [?] [,][8]

   Enter HORATIO, [BARNARD,] *and* MARCELLUS [BARNARDO][9]

HAM. I am glad to see you [*well*] [dele] C.

p. 275.   HAM. I would not [*have*] your enemy say so [heare][10] C.
col. 1. To [*take*] it truster of your owne report [make][11]

HOR. Indeed my Lord, it [*followeth*] hard upon [followed][12]

I [*should*] not looke upon his like againe [shall][13]

HAM. Saw? Who? [Saw whom.][14]

Within his Truncheon's length ; whilst they [*bestill'd*] [bechill'd] C.

[1] Warburton. [2] 4to 1604. [3] 4tos. [4] 4tos. [5] 4tos. [6] Theobald. [7] Variorum. [8] Variorum
[9] 4to 1604. [10] 4tos. [11] 4tos & fol. 1623. [12] 4tos & fol. 1623. [13] 4to & fol. 1623. [14] Johnson.

Printed Text of Folio 1632.	*MS. Corrections.*
It lifted up it‸ head	[s]¹
HOR. As I doe live my [*honourable*] Lord 'tis true	[honoured]²
col. 2. HAM. His Beard was [*grisly*]	[grisled]³ C.
Let it be [*trebble*] in your silence still	[tenable]⁴ C.
[*Froward,*] not permanent ; sweet not lasting	[Forward]⁵
The suppliance of a minute ;‸ No more	[but]
In thewes and Bulke : but as [*his*] Temple waxes	[the]⁶
The vertue of his [*feare:*] but you must feare	[will]⁷ C.
p. 276. The [*sanctity*] and health of the whole state	[safety]⁸ C.
col. 1. As he in his peculiar [*sect*] and [*force*]	[act]⁹ C. [place]⁹ C.
If with [*two*] credent eare	[too]¹⁰
And keepe [*within*] the reare of your affection	[you in]¹¹ C.
The Canker galls the [*infant*] of the Spring	[infants]¹²
Be wary th[*a*]n	[e]
As watchm[*e*]n to my heart	[a]
And re[*a*]kes not	[c]
Bear't that th' [*opposed*] may beware of thee	[opposer]¹³
Are of a most select and generous [*cheff*] in that	[choise]¹⁴ C.
[*A*] borrowing duls, &c.	[And]¹⁵
col. 2. [*Roaming*] it thus, you'l tender me a foole	[Running] C.
OPHE. And hath given countenance to‸ his speech	[it in] afterwards part. oblit.
My Lord, with all the‸ vowes of heaven	[holy]¹⁶
You must not take for fire. [*For*] this time, Daughter	[From]¹⁷
Not of the [*eye,*] &c.	[dye]¹⁸ C.
Breathing like sanctified and pious [*bonds*]	[bawds]¹⁹ C.
[Doe not beleeve his vowes ; for they are Broakers	Crossed out
to	
The better to beguile. This is for all]	

¹ 3rd 4to.   ² 4tos & fol. 1623.   ³ 4tos.   ⁴ 4tos.   ⁵ 4tos.   ⁶ Hanmer.   ⁷ 4tos.   ⁸ 4to 1604.
⁹ 4tos.   ¹⁰ 4tos and fol. 1623.   ¹¹ 4tos.   ¹² 4to, 1604, & fol. 1623.   ¹³ 3rd 4to.   ¹⁴ Steevens.
¹⁵ 4tos & fol. 1623.   ¹⁶ 4to 1604.   ¹⁷ 4tos.   ¹⁸ 4tos.   ¹⁹ Theobald.

| *Printed Text of Folio* 1632. | *MS. Corrections.* |

Have you so [*slander*] any [*moment*] leisure   [squander] C. [moments]¹ C.

Look too't, I charge you ;ₐ come your way   [so now] C.

ₐ

Enter HAMLET, HORATIO, MARCELLUS.   [Sc. 4]²

p. 277, What does this meane my Lord ?ₐ   [*Chambers*] Chambers also in
col. 1.   pencil on outer margin.

And as he dr[*e*]ines his draughts   [a]³

*Enter Ghost.*ₐ   [*armed as before*] [armed] oc-
                                            curs also in pencil on the

Be thy e[*v*]ents wicked or charitable   [nt]⁴ C.   [outer margin.

King, Father, Royall Dane : Oh [*oh*] answer me   [dele]⁵

With thoughts beyond [*thee ; reaches*]   [the reaches]⁶

Or to the dreadfull S[*onnet*] of the Cliffe   [ummit]⁷ C.

Which might deprive your Soveraignty of Reason

This line had been corrected into

[Which might deprive you of your Soveraign Reason]

but the corr. afterwards partially obliterated.

HOR. Be rul'd, you shall not goe.ₐ   [*They struggle*]

col. 2.   HOR. Heavenₐ will direct it.   [s]

And for the day confin'd to [*fast in*] fi[*er*]s   [lasting]⁸ C. [re] but after-
                                                         wards obliterated.
                                                         Opposite to the correction *lasting*
                                                         is the following pencil note:
                                                         "See LLL 133. This is in
                                                         Smith's . . . . 1765."

To eares of Flesh and Blood ; list Hamleₐ, [*oh*] list   [t] [dele]

With witchraft of his wit[*s*], [*ha*]th traiterous gifts   [dele] [wi]⁹ C.

p. 278, But soft, methinks I scent the Morning[*s*] Ayre   [dele]¹⁰
col. 1. Of Life, of Crowne, and Queene at once [*dispatcht*]   [despoiled] C.

Cut off even in the blossom[*es*]   [dele]

And shall I couple hell ? Oh fie : hold [*my*] heart   [dele] C.

---

¹ 3rd 4to. ² Rowe. ³ 4to 1604. ⁴ 4tos. ⁵ 4tos. ⁶ 4tos. ⁷ Rowe. ⁸ Heath. ⁹ 4tos & var. ¹⁰ 4tos.

Printed Text of Folio 1632.	*MS. Corrections.*
Unmixt with baser matter ; [*yes,*] yes, by heaven ⁚	[dele][1]
Oh most pernicious_Λ woman	[and perfidious] C. *perfidious* in pencil can be seen underneath the ink.
At least I'm sure it may be so in Denmarke_Λ	[wri . .][2] afterwards oblit.

Enter HORATIO *and* MARCELLUS.   [*lower down*]

MAR. How ist't my Noble Lord ?   [*Enter*]

col. 2. HOR. These are but wilde & hur[*l*]ing words, my [t]
    Lord.

HOR. What is't my Lord ?_Λ we will   [‖Mar.]

GHO. Sweare.   [*vnder*]

GHO. Sweare.   [*vnder*]

Than [*are*] dream't of in [*our*] Philosophy   The two *italic* words have been crossed through, the crossing afterwards obliterated.

With Armes encombred thus, or th[*u*]s, head shake   [i][3]

Or such ambiguous giving_Λ out to note   [s][4]

p. 279, GHOST. Sweare.   [*vnder*]

col. 1. With all my love_Λ commend me to you   [I doe][5] pencil underneath.

Actus Secundus   [*Scœna prima*]
    Λ

POLON. You shall doe marvel_Λs wisely.   [ou][6] also in pencil.

A[*nd*] thus, I know his father and his friends,   [s][7] C. *s* also in pencil.

    [REYNOLD. As gaming my Lòrd   These lines crossed through in ink, also marked in pencil.
          to

Reynol. I my Lord, I would know that]

[*Polon.*] Marry Sir, here's my drift   [dele]

col. 2 [*Reynol.*] At closes in the consequence, I marry, [Pol.][8]

---

[1] 4to 1604. [2] Rowe. [3] 4tos, 1603, 1604-5. [4] Warburton. [5] 4tos & fol. 1623. [6] 4to 1605.
[8] 4tos. [9] 4to 1604 & fol. 1623.

Printed Text of Folio 1632.	*MS. Corrections.*

The[*ir*] falling out at Tennis [re][1]

I saw him enter such a house of sa[*i*]le ; [dele][2]

Your bait of falshood, takes this Ca[*p*]e of truth ; [rp][3] C.

He rais'd a sigh, so [*hid*]eous and profound [pit][4]

p. 280, col. 1. I am sorry that with better [*sp*]eed and judgement [h][5] C.

I had not quoted him. I fear[*e*] he did but trifle [d][6]

col. 2. My Newes shall be the [*Newes*] to that great Feast [fruite][7] C.

KING. Thyselfe doe grace to them, and bring them in.ᴀ [*Exit Pol.*][8]

KING. Well, we shall sift him. Welcome ᴀ good [my][9]
Friends

With an intreaty herein further shewneᴀ [(*letter*)]

Meane time we thanke you for your well-[*look't*] [took][10]

POL. This businesse is [*very*] well ended [dele][11] C.

My Liege and Mad[*r*]m [a][12]

p. 281, col. 1. That we find out [*the*] the cause of this effect [dele][13]

Hath given me this : now gather, and surmiseᴀ [*reades*][14]

Thats an ill Phrase, a vil[*d*]e Phrase, beautified [dele][15]

is a vil[*d*]e [dele][16]

And more above hath his solicitingᴀ, [s][17]

Or my deere Majesty youᴀ Queene [r][18]

Into the Madnesse where[*o*]n [i][19]

And [*all*|*we*] waile for [2. 1.] C.

He walkes fo[*u*]r[*e*] houres together [dele][20] C.

p. 281, col. 2. QUEE. So he [*has*] indeed [doth][21]

[*And*] keepe a Farme and Carters [But][22] C.

One man pick'd out of [*two*] thousand [ten][23] C.

---

[1] 4to 1604 & fol. 1623. [2] 4to 1604. [3] 4tos. [4] 4tos & fol. 1623. [5] 4tos. [6] 4tos.
[7] 4tos. [8] Rowe. [9] 4tos. [10] 4tos & fol. 1623. [11] 4tos. [12] 4tos & fol. 1623. [13] 4tos.
[14] Variorum. [15] 4tos. [16] 4tos. [17] 4tos [18] 4tos & fol. 1623. [19] 4tos. [20] Hanmer. [21] 4tos.
[22] 4tos. [23] 4tos.

Printed Text of Folio 1632.	*MS. Corrections.*
HAM. [For if the Sun breed Magots in a dead	
dogge, being a good kissing Carrion]	[*dele*]
[POL. I have my Lord.]	[*dele*]
[HAM. Let her not walke i'th Sunne:	
Conception is a blessing, but not	
as your daughter may conceive.	[*dele*]
Friend, looke too 't.]	
POL. How say you by that &c.‸	[*to himselfe*]¹
What doe you read my Lord?‸	[*to him*]
POL. I meane the matter you [*meane*]	[reade]²
purging thicke Amber, [*or*] Plum-Tree	[and]³
l[*o*]cke of Wit,	[a]⁴
How pregnant (sometimes) his Replies are‸	[*to himselfe*]¹
My honorable Lord, I will most humbly	[*him*]
HAM.‸ These tedious old fooles	[*Enter*]
POLON. You goe to seeke my Lord Hamlet, there	
he is‸	[*Exit*]⁵
HAM. Nor the soales of her Shooe‸?	[s]
[GUILD. Faith, her privates, we]	[*dele*]
HAM. [In the secret parts of Fortune? Oh, most	
true: she is a Strumpet.]	[*dele*]
[GUILD. Which dreames indeed are ambition	
to	[*dele*]
Heroes the Beggers Shadowes:]	
prevent your discovery [*of*] your secrecy	[and]⁶
it goes so heav[*en*]ly with my disposition	[i] C.⁷
this brave ore-hanging‸ this Majesticall	[firmam^t]⁸ C.
golden fire‸; why, it appear[*ed*]	[s] [s]⁹
though by your smiling‸	[*Smile, R.*]

p. 282, col. 1. (margin)

col. 2. (margin)

---

¹ These *asides* are as old as Rowe.   ² 4tos.   ³ 4tos.   ⁴ 4tos.   ⁵ Rowe.   ⁶ 4tos.   ⁷ 4tos.
4tos.   ⁹ Var.

Printed Text of Folio 1632.	*MS. Corrections.*
[HAM. How chances it they travaile	
to	[dele]
if Philosophy could find it out.]	
p. 283, HAM. Then ca[*n*] each Actor on his Asse.	[me][1] C.
col. 1. [POLO. The best Actors in the world, either for Tragedy	[dele]
to	*Pans* has however been made
the [*Pans*] Chanson will shew you more]	into [pious][2] C.
col. 2. twas Cau[*t*]ary	[i][3]
there was no [*Sallets*] in the lines	[Salt][4] C.
but it was (as I [*re*]ccived it	[con] but partially obliterated.
One [*chiefe*] speech in it	[dele][5] C.
Blacke as h[*e*] purpose	[is][6]
When h[*is*] lay	[e][7]
p. 284, And lik'[*d*] a Newtrall	[e][8]
col. 1. Breake all the Spokes and F[*a*]llies	[e][9]
About her lanke and all ore-te[*a*]med Loynes	[e][10]
And passion‸ [*in*] the Gods	[ate][11] C. [dele] C.
according totheir des[*a*]rt	[e][12]
You are welcome to Elsonower‸	[*Exeunt Players*]
col. 2. Make mad the guilty, and apal[*e*] the free	[l][13]
Like John a-d‸eames	[r][14]
To make [*Opp*]ression bitter	[transg] C.
Wh[*o*]? What an Asse am I? [*I sure*]	[y][15] C. [dele]
Ile [*r*]ent him to the quicke	[t][16]
Wherein Ile catch the Conscience of the King	
‸	[*Act* 3. *Scene* 1.]
p. 285, ROSIN. Niggard of question, but [*of*] our demands [to][17] C.	
col. 1.	

[1] 4tos.   [2] 4to 1604-5.   [3] 4tos & fol. 1623.   [4] Pope.   [5] 4tos.   [6] 4tos & fol. 1623.   [7] 4tos and fol. 1623.   [8] 4tos & fol. 1623.   [9] Variorum.   [10] Variorum.   [11] Hanmer & Capell read *passioned.* 4tos & fol. 1623.   [12] 4to 1604.   [13] Rowe.   [14] 4tos and fol. 1623.   [15] 4tos.   [16] 4tos.   [17] Made up from Hanmer and Warburton.

Printed Text of Folio 1632.	*MS. Corrections.*
[We are oft too blame in this	[dele] The passage has never-
to	theless been corrected, in two
Oh heavy burthen !]	instances.
And pious Action, we doe [*surge*] ore	[suger]¹
King. Oh 'tis true.ᴧ	[*Aside*]²
[Pol.] I heare him comming	[dele]
Enter Hamlet.ᴧ	[*Ophelia behinde reading*]
The Oppressors wrong, the [*poore*] mans Contumely	[proud]³ C.
col. 2. The pangs of [*disprized*] Love	first made into [misprized,] the *m* afterwards obliterated, and the word made [dispized]⁴ C.
Who would [*these*] Fardles beare	[dele]⁵
from whose Boᴧrne	[u]⁶
Oph. Good my Lord, ᴧ	[*forward*]
Ophe. Could beauty my lord, have	
better Comerce then [*your*] honesty ?	[with]⁷ C.
[For vertue cannot so inocculate our	
old stocke, but we shall rellish of it.]	[dele]
With more offences at my b[*e*]cke	[a] C.
play the Foole no [*way*]	[where]⁸ C.
p. 286, [Goe, farewell, Or if thou wilt needs marry	
col. 1. *to*	[dele]
the rest shall keepe as they are]	
notwithstanding corrected as follows :—	
Ham. I have heard of your [*pratl*]ing	[paint]⁹
God has given you one [*p*]ace	[f]C.¹⁰

---

¹ 4tos. ² Pope. ³ 4tos. ⁴ 4tos 1604-5. ⁵ 4tos. ⁶ Pope. ⁷ 4tos. ⁸ 4tos. ⁹ Theobald ; 4tos. *paintings.* ¹⁰ 4tos.

Printed Text of Folio 1632.	*MS. Corrections.*
[*gidge*]	[gigge][1] C.
all but one shall₄	[live][2] C.
That unmatch'd for[*tun*]e	[m][3]
Whereon his brain[*es*]	[brain] C.
₄	[*Scene 2*]

p. 286,   *Enter* HAMLET & *two or three of the Players.*   [*unreadie*]
col. 2.

too much₄ your hand thus	[with][4] C.
Su[*r*]e the Action to the word	[t][5]
That you ore-st[*o*]p not	[e][6] C.
[*or*] [Nor man]	[dele] [nor man][7] C.
Exe₄nt Players	[*u*][8]
HAM. Bid the Players make hast₄.	[e]
HAM. What hoa, Horatio₄.	[*Enter* Ho.][9]
As ere my Conv[*s*]er₄ation	[dele] [s][10]

p. 287,   [Why should the poore be flatterd   [dele]   The line, however,
col. 1.   *to*   " corrected "

As I doe thee. Something too much of this.]	
And crooke the pregnant Hindges of the Knee	[begging] in pencil
Even with the₄Comment of [*my*] soule	[very][11] C. [thy][11] C.
As Vulcans Styth₄. Give him [*n*]eedful note	[y][12] [h][12] C.
And after we will both our judgement₄ joyne	[s][13]
₄*Enter* KING, QUEENE, POLONIUS, &c.	[*Sennet*]
[*his*] Guard carrying Torches	[a][14]
Get you a place	
	[*Enter*]
₄	
POLO. Oh ho, doe you marke that ?₄	[*Goes to O*φ*elia*]

---

[1] 4tos.   [2] 4tos & fol. 1623.   [3] 4tos & fol. 1632.   [4] 4tos.   [5] 4tos & fol. 1623.   [6] 4tos.   [7] 4tos.
[8] This direction is first found in 4to 1603.   [9] 4to 1604.   [10] 4tos & fol. 1623.   [11] 4tos & fol.
1623.   [12] 4tos.   [13] 4tos & fol. 1623.   [14] Jennens.

Printed Text of Folio 1632.	*MS. Corrections.*
[HAM. Lady, shall I lye in your Lap	
to	[dele]
HAM. Nothing]	
OPHE. I my Lord‸	[*Lie downe neare her*]
col. 2. HAM. Let the Divell weare blacke	
for Ile have [*a*] suite of Sables	[no]
[OPHE. Will they tell us what this shew meant	
to	[dele]
Ile ma‸ke the Play.]	[r][1]
Enter ‸ KING, *and his* QUEENE.	[*Player*][2]
Phœbus Car[*t*]	[r] C.[3]
World have time‸ twelve	[s][4]
p. 288, And as my love is [*siz,*] my feare is so.	Apparently first corrected into
col. 1.	[*fix'd*] afterwards obliterated
	and made [siz'd][5] C.
The violence of [*o*]ther Griefe or joy	[ei][6]
Directly [*seasons*] him his Enemy	[p . . .s] but obliterated
HAM. If she should breake [*it now*]	[her vow] C.
col. 2. [HAM. I could interpret betweene you and your love	
to	[dele]
HAM. So you [*mis*]take husbands]	[must][7]
HAM. Why let the str[*u*]cken Deere goe weepe	[i][8]
[Would not this Sir, and a Forrest of Feathers	
to	[dele]
HORA. You might have Rim'd]	
Provinciall Roses on my ra[*c*]'d shoes	[ais][9] C.
[*Ham.*] Oh good Horatio	[dele]

---

[1] 4tos & fol. 1623. [2] Pope. [3] Rowe. [4] 4tos & fol. 1623. [5] fol. 1623. 3rd and 4th folios have *fix'd*. So Rowe and Pope. [6] 4tos. [7] Theobald. [8] 4to 1603. [9] Steevens.

<table>
<tr><td>Printed Text of Folio 1632.</td><td>MS. Corrections.</td></tr>
</table>

p. 289, So wildly from [*my*] affaire	[the] C.
col. 1. You doe [*freely*] barre the doore of your owne	[surely][1] C.
col. 2. In this little Organe, yet cannot you make it‸	[speake][2] C.
POLON. By th' M[*i*]sse.	[a][3]
Tis now the very witching time of night,‸	[*Exeunt*]
How in my words so[*m*]ever she be shent	[dele][4]
‸	[Scene 3]

Enter KING, ROSINCROSS, & GUILDERSTAR.

To keepe those‸ many bodies safe	[verie] C.
[the cease of Majesty	
to	[dele]
Did the King sighe, but with a general grone]	
Fixt on the Som[*ne*]t of the highest Mount	[mi][5]
Are mortiz'd and adjo‸n'd	[i][6]
p. 290, In the corrupted curr[*a*]nts of this world	[e][7]
col. 1. And oft tis seene, the wicked p[*rize*] it selfe	[urse] C.
All may be well.‸	[*Kneeles*]

Enter HAMLET.‸

	‸ [(*behind*) *his sword drawen*]
col. 2. my thoughts remaine below.‸	[*rising*]
S[*o*]ree'nd	[c][8]
Ile [*sile*]nce me [*en'e*] heere	[sco][9] C. [even][9] C.
Withdraw, I heare him comming.‸	[*Exit Pol. behind the arras*]
HAM. Goe, goe, you question with an [*idle*] tongue	[wicked][10] C.
QUEE. Nay, then Ile se[*t*] those to you	[nd] C.
You goe not till I set‸ up a glasse	[you][11]

---

[1] 4tos; *surely but,* variorum.   [2] 4tos.   [3] 4tos.   [4] 4th 4to.   [5] Rowe, &c.   [6] 4tos & fol. 1623.
[7] 4tos.   [8] 4tos & fol. 1623.   [9] Hanmer and Warburton.   [10] 4tos.   [11] 4tos & fol. 1623.

Printed Text of Folio 1632.	*MS. Corrections.*
Pol. What hoa, helpe, helpe, helpe._Λ	[*within*]
Pol. Oh I am slaine. *Killes Polonius.*	[*at the backe and then comes forward*]
Quee. As kill[*d*] a King?	[dele]¹
Ham. I Lady, twas my word	[*Seeing Polonius*]
Leave wringing of your hands, peace, sit you downe	[(*to her*)]
See what a grace_Λ seated on his Brow	[was]²
N[*o*]w lighted on a	[e]³
Heere is your husband, like a Mildew'd [*d*]eare	[dele]⁴
Blasting his wholesome br[*eath*]	[other]⁵ C.
Would st[*e*]p from this	[oo] C.
When the compulsive Ard[*u*]r[*e*]	[o]⁶
A[*s*] Reason panders Will	[nd]⁷ C.

p. 291, col. 1.

Enter Ghost_Λ	[*unarmed*]
That laps't in [*Ti*]me and Passion.	[fu] C.
And with [*the*] corporall ayre	[th' in]⁸ C.
Start_Λ up and stand_Λ an end	[s] [s]⁹
Looke where he goes even now out at the Portall. *Exit*_Λ	[*Ghost*]¹⁰
And doe not spred the Compost o[*r*] the Weedes	[n]¹¹
Thus bad begins, and worse remaines behind_Λ	[*to himself*] but almost oblit.
And breath of life : I have no life to breath_Λ	[e]¹²
	[*Exit Queene*]

col. 2.

p. 292, col. 1.

Λ

Exit Hamlet *tugging in* Polonius.	[*IIII Act* 4. *Sc.* 1.]¹³
	[dele]
There's matter[*s*]	[dele]¹⁴ nearly obliterated.
Ore whom his very madnesse, like some O[*a*]re	[dele]¹⁵
But we will ship him hence, and this vil[*d*]e deed	

---

¹ 4tos. ² 4tos & fol. 1623. ³ 4tos & fol. 1623. ⁴ 4tos & fol. 1623. ⁵ 4tos. ⁶ Rowe, &c. ⁷ 4tos. ⁸ 4tos. ⁹ 3rd & 4th 4tos. ¹⁰ 4to 1604. ¹¹ 4tos. ¹² Rowe, &c. ¹³ Rowe. ¹⁴ 4tos & fol. 1623. ¹⁵ 4tos.

Printed Text of Folio 1632.	*MS. Corrections.*

p. 292,
col. 2.

Enter ^AKing.

[*Scene* 2.]

Who like not in their judgement_A, but their eyes :

[s]

But ne[*ar*]er

[v]¹ C.

HAM.   a certaine convocation

of_A wormes are ene at him

[palated] C.

[KING. What dost thou meane by this ?]

[dele]

p. 293,
col. 1.

[HAM. Nothing but to shew you —— gut of a
Begger]

[dele]

HAM. He will stay till ye come _A

[*Exeunt*]²

HAM. [I see a Cherube that sees him

[dele]

but,] [*c*]ome

[C]

Payes homage to us; thou maist not coldly se[*t*]

[e]

How ere my h[*a*]p_As,

[o] [e]³ C.

[*Enter* FORTINBRAS *with an Army.*

[*Scene* 3.]

to

FOR. Goe safely on.]

[dele]

Enter ^AQUEENE *and* HORATIO.

[*Scene* 4 3.]

col. 2. At his head a [*grass*|-greene*] Turfe

[2. 1.] C.

Let in the Maid, [*let in*] a Maid, never departed more

[that out]⁴

p. 294,
col. 1. [*Keep*]es on his wonder, keepes himselfe in cloudes

This has been crossed through,
but the margin on which the
correction is made has been
carefully torn away.*

---

¹ 4tos.   ² Variorum.   ³ Johnson suggested *hopes*, and that the passage should rhyme ; and
the folio, 1623, has—*were ne'er begun.*   ⁴ 4tos & fol. 1623.

* In the *Complete List* we are told by Mr. Collier that the " corrected " Folio has "*Feeds* for *Keepes ;*" *Feeds*
being the reading of the 4tos. Consequently the margin must have been intentionally mutilated *since* 1856, when
the *List* was published, in order to get rid of the reading of the 4tos ! Similar instances of recent mutilation occur
throughout the " Folio."

Printed Text of Folio 1632.	*MS. Corrections.*
*Enter a Messenger*_ᴧ	[*Enter*]
Let them guard the door. What is the matter ?	[*in haste*]

p. 294.
col. 2.

Ore-beares your officers[,] the rabble call him [*Lord*]	[:] [King] C.
The Ratifiers & props of every wor[*d*]	Altered but obliterated.
KING. The doores are broke.	[*Sword out*]
Even here betweene the chaste unsmi[*t*]ched brow	[r]¹
[KING. Good Laertes	
to	[dele] but the following correc-
Repast them with my blood]	tions nevertheless made.
Of your deare fathers death, [*if*] writ in yʳ revenge	[is't]² C.
That S_ᴧoop-stake	[w]
KING. Why now ? [*what noyse is that ?*]	[you speake]
Enter OPHELIA_ᴧ.	[*still distraught*]
[Nature is fine in Love	
to	[dele]
After the thing it loves.]	
And on his grave raine[*s*] many a teare	[dele]
No, no, he is dead, go_ᴧe to [*thy*] Death-bed	[n] C. [his] C.
His Beard _ᴧas white as Snow	[w] C.³

p. 295,
col. 1.

And o[*f*] all Christian Soules, I pray God	[n]⁴
God buy ye. *Exit* OPHELIA_ᴧ.	[*dauncing distracted*]
Be you content to lend your pa_ᴧience	[t]⁵
ᴧ	[*Scene ⅔, 4.*]

col. 2.

Enter HORATIO, *with an Attendant.*	
SAY. God bless you[*r*] Sir	[dele]⁶
[*Stood*] Challenger on mount of all the Age	[Sole] C.
KING. Laertes you shall _ᴧthem	[heare]⁷

---

¹ 4tos & fol. 1623.   ² 4tos.   ³ 4tos.   ⁴ Johnson.   ⁵ 4tos & fol. 1623.   ⁶ 4tos & fol. 1623.
⁷ 4tos & fol. 1623.

H

Printed Text of Folio 1632.	*MS. Corrections.*

Or is it some abuse ?   [*Or*] no such thing   [and][1] C.
And for his death no wind of blame
   shall breath_ᴧ.   [e][2]

p. 296, Had witchcraft in't ; he grew [*i*]nto his Seat   [u][3]
col. 1.
And Iemme of all [*our*] Nation   [that][4]
If one could match you [*Sir.*]   This report of his   [dele][5]
Did Hamlet so envenom with hi[*s*] Envy   [r]
Your sodaine comming [*over*] to play with him   [o'er][6]
   LAER. Wh[*y*] out of this, my Lord   [at][7] C.
A Sword unba[*i*]ted   [dele][8]
Requit_ᴧ him for your Father   [e][9]
And for that purpose I'll annoi[*o*]t my Sword   [n][10]
So mortall, [*I*] but dip[*t*] a knife in it   [that][11] C. [dele][11] C.
Wee'l make a solemne wager on your co[*mm*]ings   [n n][12] C.
col. 2. As make your bowts more violent to th⌊*e*⌋ end   [at][13]
Or like a creature Native, and [*d*]educed   [r] *r* also in pencil at side. C.
Pull'd the poore wretch from her melodious [*b*]y   [la][14] C.

           ᴧ   [*V. Act 5, Scene* 1.][15]

     Enter two Clownes _ᴧ   [*with Spades & tooles.*]

    and an Act hath three branches :
It is [*an*] Act   [to][16] C.
   OTHER. Nay but he_ᴧre you, Goodman Delver   [a][17]
p. 297, [OTHER. Was he a Gentleman
col. 1.
        to   [dele]
   OTHER. Goe to.]

----

[1] 4tos. [2] Rowe, and all after. [3] 4tos.   In the Complete List *the* is given as the reading : *the* is also the reading of the quartos. [5] 4tos & fol. 1623. [6] 4tos & fol. 1623. [7] 4tos. [8] 4tos. [9] 4tos & fol. 1623. [10] 4tos & fol. 1623. [11] 4tos. [12] 4tos [13] 4tos. [14] 4tos. [15] Rowe. [16] 4tos. [17] 4tos & fol. 1623.

Printed Text of Folio 1632.	*MS. Corrections.*
Get thee to [*Yaugan,*] fetch me a	[You']¹
sto[*a*] pe Liquor	[o]²
Sings [*and digges.*] ᴧ	[*Exit other Clo.*]³
Clowne sings ᴧ	[(*Skull*)]

But age, &c.

col. 2. *Clowne sings* ᴧ   [(*Skull*)]

A Picke-axe, &c.

HAM.   or equivocation will

[*follow*] us   [undoe]⁴

[How long hast thou been a Grave-maker?

to   [dele]

Its no great matter there.]

p. 298, [HAM. Why
col. 1.   to   [dele]

Man and Boy thirty yeeres.]

A Tanner will last you nine yeere[*s*]   [dele]⁵

Alexander returne[*th*] into dust   [d]

Should patch a Wall, ᴧexpell the Winter's flaw   [t']⁶

*with*ᴧ *Lords attendant*   [*Priest and*]⁷

col. 2. Foredoe it ᴧ owne life; [*t*]was some Estate   [s]⁸ [it]⁸

Couch we a while, and marke,   [*At one side*]

To sing sa[*ge*] Requiem   [d] C.

QUEEN. Sweets, to the sweet farewell ᴧ   [*Flowers*]

LAER. Oh, t[*er*]r[*i*]ble wooe[*r*]   [dele] [e] C. [dele]⁹ C.

---

¹ Yon *Complete List.* ² fol. 1623, and subsequent editions read *stoup* or *stoop.* ³ Rowe.
⁴ 4tos & fol. 1623. ⁵ 4tos & fol. 1623. ⁶ 4tos & fol. 1623. ⁷ *Priest* in all modern editions.
⁸ 4th 4to. ⁹ 4tos.

Printed Text of Folio 1632.	MS. Corrections.
H AM. What is he, whose griefes ˄	[*Forward*]
LAER. The Divell take thy soule ˄	[*Seize him*]¹
Sir though I am not spleen[*ative*] and rash	[eticke]
Which let thy wisenesse feare. Away thy hand˄	[*Strive*]
Woo't weepe ? woo't fight ? woo't ˄ teare thy selfe ?	[storme or] C.
p. 299, Ile doo't˄. Dost thou come here to whine col. 1.	[Ile doo't] C.
˄ Anon as patient as the female Dove	[QUEENE]²
The Cat will mew, [*and*] Dog will have his day	[the]³ C.
Strengthen you˄ patience in our last nights speech	[r]⁴ [*Exit*]
Wee'l put the matter to the present push˄	[*To Laertes*]
	Scene 2.⁵
˄ *Enter* HAMLET *and* HORATIO.	
[me thought I lay	[dele] corrected however as
to HOR. That is most certaine.]	follows.
(And praise [*be*] rashnesse for it) let us [*know*]	[to] oblit. [owne] C.
When our de[*are*] plots do [*paule*]	[epe]⁶ C. [faile]⁷ C.
[HAM.] Up from my Cabin.	[dele]
(My [*t*]eares forgetting manners)	[f]⁸
No not to stay the grin[*g*]ding of the Axe	[dele]⁹
But wilt thou heare, how I did proceed ?˄	[*Giving it*]
The effect[*s*] of what I wrote	[dele]¹⁰
And many such like Ass[*i*]s of great charge	[e]¹¹
col. 2. Subscrib'd it, gau'˄ th' Impression	[e]¹²
Was our Sea-fight, and what to this was se[*ment*]	[quell] C.¹³
They are not neere my conscience ; their de[*b*]ate	[fe]¹⁴ C.
Tis dangerous when ˄ baser nature comes	[a]

¹ Rowe. ² 4tos. ³ Theobald. ⁴ 4tos. ⁵ Rowe. ⁶ 4tos. ⁷ Pope. ⁸ 4tos & fol. 1623.
⁹ 4tos & fol. 1623. ¹⁰ 4tos. ¹¹ The suggested quibble of *asses* is Johnson's. ¹² 3rd and 4th folios.
¹³ 4tos read *sequent*. ¹⁴ 4tos.

Printed Text o Folio 1632.	*MS. Corrections.*
HAM. Does it not, think'st th[*ee*]	[ou][1]
Throwne out │his Angle for my proper life	[2] C.
[dost know this waterfly	
to	[dele]
spacious in the possession of dirt.]	
OSR. Swe‸t Lord, if your [*friend*]ship	[e][2] [lord][2] C.
were at leasure	
p. 300, He hath on[*e*] twelve for mine	[dele][3]
col. 1. [*Ile*] gaine nothing but my shame	[I]
[he does well to	
commend it himselfe	[dele]
to	the line however corrected.
the Bubbles are out.]	
there are no tongues else for's [*tongue*]	[turne][4] C.
but thou wouldest not thinke	
how‸ all heere	[ill is][5] C.
HOR. If your mind dislike any thing, obey‸	[it][6]
col. 2. HAM. Give me your pardon, Sir, I've	
done you wrong‸	[*To Laertes*]
[Was't *Hamlet* wrong'd *Laertes*? Never, *Hamlet*.	
to	[dele]
His Madnesse is poore *Hamlets* enemy]	
And hurt my [*M*]other	[Br][7] C.
LAER. Come one for me‸	[*Bring foiles*]
KING. Set me the Sto‸pes of Wine upon that Table	[o][8]
And in the Cup an union shall [*h*]e throw‸	[b] [ne] but obliterated.
p. 301, The Cannons to the Heavens, the Heaven‸ to Earth	[s][9]
col. 1.	

---

[1] Rowe.　[2] 4tos.　[3] 4tos.　[4] 4tos.　[5] 4tos.　[6] 4tos.　[7] 4tos.　[8] 4tos.
[9] 3rd 4to.

Printed Text of Folio 1632.	*MS. Corrections.*

HAM. Ile play this bout first ; set⌃ by a while   [it]¹ C.

Here'[s] a Napkin, rub thy browes⌃   [is] C. [my sonne] C.

   QU. I will my Lord.⌃   [*She drinkes*]²

   KING. Part them ; they are incens'd.⌃   [*Both wounded*]

   HOR. They bleed on both sides. How is'[t] my Lord. [it]³

To my⌃ Sprindge, Osricke   [owne]⁴ C.

I am poyson'd.⌃   [*dies*]⁵

p. 301,   (*as this fell Sergeant death*   [dele] obliterated.
col. 2.   *Is strick't in this Arrest*) oh I could tell you⌃   [all] obliterated.

   HOR. Never beleeve it.   [*takes the Cup.*]

Let go, by heaven I'le have't.   [*Struggling, Hamlet gets it.*]
       The word *struggling* afterwards
       in part obliterated.

Good night [*sweet Prience*]   [be blest] [Finis.]

[Why do's the Drumme come hither

         to   [dele] a line however corrected.

To tell him his command'ment is fulfill'd]

[*His*] quarry cries on Havocke   [This]⁶ C.

p. 302,   These two columns crossed
cols. 1   through [dele], but neverthe-
& 2.   less the following alterations
col. 1. I have some Ri⌃ t[e]s of memory in this Kingdome   [gh] [dele]⁷   [made.

col. 2. Which [*are*] to claime, my vantage doth   [now]⁸ C.

   HOR. Of that I shall [*alwayes*] cause to speake   [have also]⁹

But let this s[*ame*] be presently perform'd   [cene] C.

   [While I remaine behind to tell
   a tale

   That shall hereafter turne the
   hearers pale.]

---

¹ 4tos.   ² Capell.   ³ Variorum.   ⁴ 4tos.   ⁵ All modern editions from Rowe.   ⁶ 4tos.
⁷ 4tos.   ⁸ 4tos.   ⁹ 4tos.

Collation of a page taken from Henry VI. Part II.

Corrected folio, p. 142.   Collier, 1856, p. 223, col. 2.   *MS. Corrections.*

What say ye, Countrimen ? will ye [*relent*]   [repent] C.
Or let a [*rabble*]   [rebell]
col. 1. Shake he his weapon at us, and passe by.   [As he doth passe us let his
                                                              weapon shake.] partially
                                                              obliterated.

   given [*out*] these arms   [up] obliterated.
Henry hath mony[,] you are strong and [*manly*]   [;] [crye]
God on our side, [*we*] doubt not [*of*] Victorie   [dele] obliterated.
Follow me souldiers wee'l devise a [*meane*]   [thing] obliterated.
col. 2. Was ever king that [*joy'd*] an earthly Throne   [filled] obliterated.
   [*in*]fortunate   [unfortunate] obliterated.
And with a puissant and [*a mighty*] power   [united] C.
Like to a Ship, that having scap'd a Tempest
Is straightway [*claim'd*] and boorded with a Pyrate.   [calm'd]
Of gallow-glasses and stout ᴀ Kernes   [Irish] C.
I pray thee, Buckingham, go ᴀ and meet him*   [thou] C
Come wife, let's in and learne to [*governe better*]   [rule againe] obliterated.

---

* In *Complete List*, Mr. Collier incorrectly printed—
I pray thee, Buckingham, then go and meet him.

Mr. Collier will perhaps be able to explain how so small a proportion of the marginal corrections of the " Folio " is recorded in his *List*, in which he informs us he can " safely assert that no sin of omission can be discovered."

I now proceed to examine the only other ground put forward by Mr. Collier in proof of the authority of his "Folio," viz., *that it, with all its corrections, had been in the possession of Mr. Parry some half-century ago.* This assertion he first made in the Preface to the second edition of *Notes and Emendations*, 1853, and confirmed by the affidavit of 1856.

Had such been actually the case, it would of course have relieved the present generation from the suspicion of having perpetrated this " most discreditable fraud." But, as we shall presently see, Mr. Parry altogether denies having ever possessed this volume, and states that *he had not even seen it* until the thirteenth of July in the last year (1859.)

Mr. Collier, however, asserts that the book was identified by Mr. Parry, and he gives two distinct narratives, not only of the fact but of the manner of the identification. These two narratives differ materially, if they are not actually contradictory. I subjoin both for the purpose of comparison. The first occurs in the Preface to the second edition of *Notes and Emendations*, 1853, where "the important discovery regarding the ownership and history of my corrected folio 1632" is thus related :—

"John Carrick Moore, Esq., of Hyde Park Gate, Kensington * * * was kind enough to address a note to me, in which he stated that a friend of his, a gentleman of the name of Parry, had been at one time in possession of the very folio upon which I founded my recent volume of "Notes and Emendations," that Mr. Parry had been well acquainted with the fact that its margins were filled throughout by manuscript notes, and that he accurately remembered the handwriting in which they were made On being shewn the facsimile, which accompanied my first edition, and which is repeated in the present, he declared his instant conviction that it had been copied from what had once been his folio 1632. How, or precisely when, it escaped from his custody he knew not, but the description of it in my "Introduction," exactly corresponded with his recollection.

"I lost no time in thanking Mr. Moore for these tidings, and in writing to Mr. Parry for all the particulars within his knowledge. Unfortunately the latter gentleman, just before he received my note, had met with a serious injury, which confined him to his bed, so that he was unable to send me any reply,

"For about ten days I remained in suspense, but at last I determined to wait upon Mr. Moore, to inquire

I

whether he was aware of any reason why I had not received an answer from Mr. Parry. He accounted for the silence of that gentleman on the ground of his recent accident; and as Mr. Moore was confident that Mr. Parry was correct in the conclusion that my folio 1632 had formerly belonged to him, he advised me to call upon him, being sure that he would be glad to satisfy me upon every point. I accordingly hastened to St. John's Wood, and had the pleasure of an interview with Mr. Parry, who, without the slightest reserve, gave me such an account of the book as made it certain that it was the same which, some fifty years ago, had been presented to him by a connexion of his family, Mr. George Gray. Mr. Parry described both the exterior and interior of the volume, with its innumerable corrections and its missing leaves, with so much minuteness, that no room was left for doubt."

" On the question from whence Mr. Gray, who resided at Newbury, had procured the book, Mr. Parry was not so clear and positive ; he was not in a condition to state any distinct evidence to show out of what library it had come ; but he had always understood and believed that it had been obtained, with some other old works (to the collection of which Mr. Gray was partial), from Upton Court, Berkshire,—formerly and for many years before the dispersion of the library, the residence of a Roman Catholic family of the name of Perkins, one member of which, Francis Perkins, who died in 1736, was the husband of Arabella Farmer, the heroine of the ' Rape of the Lock.'

" This information has been communicated to me so
recently, that I have not yet been able to ascertain at
what date, and in what way, the books at Upton Court
were disposed of. Mr. Parry is strongly of opinion that
Mr. Gray became the owner of this copy of the folio
1632, considerably before the end of the last century;
and Mr. Parry was himself at Upton Court about fifty
years since, when a Roman Catholic clergyman, eighty
years of age, who had remembered the books there all
his life, showed him the then empty shelves upon which
they had been placed in the library.

" A Mr. Francis Perkins died at Upton Court three
years after the publication of the folio 1632; and if
Mr. Parry's belief be correct, that the copy which
Mr. Gray gave to him had once been deposited there, it
is not impossible that Francis Perkins was the first
purchaser of it. If so, we might be led to the inference,
that either he, or one of his immediate descendants, was
the writer of the emendations; but as has been mentioned
elsewhere, the present rough calf binding was not the
original coat of the volume; and as far as my imperfect
researches have yet gone, I do not find any Thomas
Perkins recorded as of Upton Court.

" The Christian name of the great actor of the reign of
Charles I. was Richard; and a Richard Perkins, called
Esquire in Ashmole's Collections, at a date not stated,
married Lady Mervin, a benefactress of that parish.
Why should we deem it impossible that Richard Perkins
having attained eminence on the stage, subsequently
married a lady of title and property ?

"However, this and other points, dependent chiefly upon dates, remain to be investigated, and upon any of them I shall be most thankful for information.

"The only facts that I am yet able to establish are, that my folio 1632, with its elaborate corrections, about half a century since, came into the possession of Mr. Parry, from Mr. George Gray, who, it is probable, obtained it from Upton Court (about eight miles from his residence), where it is unquestionable that at an early date there was a library, likely to have contained such a book, which library was afterwards dispersed. The name of 'Tho. Perkins' on the cover, is a strong confirmation of the opinion that it once formed part of that library; and as to the identity of the volume, and hand-writing of the marginal notes, Mr. Parry feels absolutely certain.

"Having thus made, very unexpectedly, the first step (decidedly a long one), towards the history of this copy, &c., &c., it remains for me to advert to objections, &c."— (*Preface to Second Edition of "Notes and Emendations,"* 1853.)

Now I think the expressions " Mr. Parry gave me such an *account* of the book, as made it certain that it was the same which, some fifty years ago, had been presented to him by a connexion of his family;" and " Mr. Parry *described* both the exterior and interior of the volume, with its innumerable corrections and its missing leaves, with so much minuteness that no room was left for doubt," lead inevitably to the conclusion that *the book* itself was not shown to Mr. Parry. Indeed had it been, Mr. Collier would certainly have stated that fact in his narrative, as being much more conclusive as to its identification than the most minute *description* could possibly be.

In regard to Mr. Parry's account of "the exterior and interior of the volume," that gentleman and Mr. Collier are at issue. Mr. Parry asserts that he certainly recollects his volume sufficiently well to describe its appearance accurately; but that then the description could not possibly have led Mr. Collier to suppose it was the same as his corrected copy of 1632; on the contrary, it must at once have proved to him that it was wholly different, since Mr. Parry states that his volume was of the first edition, 1623, and was bound in smooth dark leather, that it had been supplied with a new back which was lettered, that there was no name of any former possessor written on the cover, and that the margins had been partially ploughed off in binding. On the other hand, Mr. Collier's folio is of the edition of 1632, is bound in rough light-coloured sheep, is neither re-backed nor lettered, the words "Tho. Perkins his Booke," are written in a bold recent hand on the upper cover, and the margins are

not mutilated.   How then, we may ask, could
Mr. Collier have possibly identified his Folio with
that formerly in the possession of Mr. Parry,
when every word of that gentleman's description
must have proved to him that the two volumes
were wholly different?

But on the 19th of July, in the present year
(1859), Mr. Collier published a second version of
the identification of the Folio, differing from, and
as seems to me, at variance with his former
narrative.   It proves at least that his memory
is treacherous, since his recollection of the facts
now are inconsistent with his statement of
them some years ago.   In the first instance,
he informed the reader that he had himself
been enabled to identify the volume by means
of Mr. Parry's *description* of it; in the second account he shifts the responsibility upon Mr. Parry,
by stating that that gentleman identified the
volume himself, by *personal inspection* of it; and
he even recounts the exact words of a conversation
which according to him took place on the occasion.
Mr. Parry however asserts that, to the best of his
belief, the circumstance thus recorded of the
volume having been shown to him never occurred;
and he further stated, in conversation with the
writer, that the incidents of his *taking* and

handing back the Folio were simply impossible, inasmuch as on the occasion alluded to he was, in consequence of an accident, halting along the road on two crutches, the management of which occupied both his hands, and must certainly have totally prevented his handling a folio volume.

Subjoined is Mr. Collier's second narrative, followed by Mr. Parry's reply to it :—

" *To the Editor of the Times.*

" SIR,—I feel most unwillingly compelled to say one other word respecting the corrected folio of Shakespeare's works in 1632, which came into my hands in 1849.

" According to Mr. Hamilton's letter, inserted in your paper of the 16th inst., Mr. Parry states that the book which he owned, and which was given to him by his relative, Mr. George Gray, about fifty years ago, was an edition different from the folio of 1632, with different corrections.

" I saw Mr. Parry twice upon the subject in the year 1853,—first at his house in St. John's Wood, when he told me (as he had previously told a common friend) that he had recognized the corrections instantly, from the fac-simile which accompanied the earliest edition of my *Notes and Emendations,* 8vo, 1852. Very soon afterwards, for greater satisfaction, I brought the corrected folio of 1632 from Maidenhead to London, and took it to St. John's Wood, but I failed to meet with Mr. Parry at home. I therefore paid a third visit to that gentleman, again carrying the book with me. I met him coming from his house, and I informed him that I had the corrected folio of 1632 under my arm, and that I was sorry he could not then examine it, as I wished. He replied,—' If you will let me see it now, I shall be able to state at once whether it was ever my book.' I therefore showed it to him on the spot, and, after looking at it in several places, he gave it back to me with these words :—' That was my book, it is the same, but it has been much ill-used since it was in my possession.'

"I took Mr. Parry's word without hesitation; and it certainly gave me increased faith in the emendations, to which I never applied a microscope or magnifying glass beyond my own spectacles. I was then living in the house of my brother-in-law; and, almost from day to day, I showed him such of the emendations of Shakespeare's text in the corrected folio of 1632 as seemed most striking or important.

"If there be upon the volume any pencillings by me, beyond crosses, ticks, and lines, they will speak for themselves; they have escaped my recollection, and, as I stated in my former letter, I have not seen the book for several years. Perhaps the microscope used by Mr. Hamilton might discover that the plumbago of my pencil was the same as that of other marks, said to be in connexion with some of the emendations.

"J. PAYNE COLLIER.

" *Maidenhead, July* 16."

"*July* 28, 1859.

" My dear Sir,—In reply to your application I have only to make the following statement, in which you will see that Mr. Collier's memory and mine are in question.

" In Mr. Collier's letter to *The Times*, printed July 19, 1859, he states that he was coming to call on me in 1853 with 'the corrected folio of 1632 under his arm,' and that he showed it to me on the road, and that I gave it back to him with these words, 'that was my book—it is the same; but it has been much ill-used since it was in my possession.'

" Now, I believe Mr. Collier to be utterly incapable of making any statement which is not strictly in accordance with his belief. I remember well meeting him, as he says, in the road, and as I was then very lame, from having hurt my knee by a fall, and was using sticks to assist me in walking, he kindly did not allow me to turn back, but walked with me in the direction I was going. I well remember some of the conversation we had during our walk; but I have not the slightest recollection that the volume of *Shakspere* was then under his arm, or of my having asserted that ' it was my book.'

" Previously to this interview with Mr. Collier he had shown me the fac-simile which he mentions in his letter, when I immediately said, on seeing it, that it was from my book. I now believe that I was mistaken, and that I was too hasty in so identifying *the volume* from a *fac-simile* of a part of a page of it. At that time Mr. Collier knew that there were several corrected folios of

K

Shakspere in existence, but he did not tell me that there were. At that time I did not know that there was any other corrected folio in existence, and I therefore supposed that Mr. Collier's fac-simile could only have been taken from my book. It was not till the 14th of this month that I learnt from Sir Frederic Madden that there are five or six corrected folios now in being, but he (Sir Frederic) did not tell me so till he had laid on the table Mr. Collier's corrected folio, and then he seemed surprised that I did not recognise it.

" Again I repeat, that having frequently since the 14th of this month, when I saw Sir Frederic Madden, tried to recollect everything about the book, I cannot remember that Mr. Collier ever showed me the book, but I well remember his showing me the fac-simile. I may be wrong, and Mr. Collier may be right.

" I have a very strong impression that *my* book was a copy of the edition of 1623, and was rather surprised when I saw Mr. Collier's ' Supplemental volume' (1853) to find that *his* book was of the edition of 1632.

" I may also add that I certainly did not tell, and could not have told Mr. Collier, that Mr. Gray ' was partial to the collection of old books,' for I believe he set no value at all on them.

" Believe me to be, my dear Sir, yours very truly,

" F. C. PARRY.

" *Mr. N. E. Hamilton, British Museum, W.C.*"

A third narrative is contained in a letter from Mr. Collier to the *Athenæum,* June 4th, 1853.* This presents some points of difference of its own,

---

* " Your readers, who have taken so lively an interest in the emendations and alterations of the text of Shakspeare contained in my copy of the folio 1632, will be glad to hear that I have just advanced an important step towards tracing the ownership and history of that remarkable book. The proof that it was in existence, in its annotated state, 50 years ago, is clear and positive ; and upon the foundation of strong probability I am able to carry it back almost to the period when the volume was published. The facts are these :—

" John Carrick Moore, Esq., of Hyde Park Gate (nephew to Sir John Moore, who fell at Corunna, in Jan. 1809), being in possession of a copy of the ' *Notes and Emendations* ' founded upon my folio 1632, happened to show it to a friend of the name of Parry, residing at St. John's Wood. Mr. Parry remarked that he had once been the owner of a folio 1632, the margins of which were much occupied by manuscript notes in an old hand-writing ; and having read my description of the book, both externally and internally, and having looked at the fac-simile which accompanied that description, he declared, without a moment's hesitation, that this very copy of the folio 1632, had been given to him about 50 years since, by Mr. George Gray, a connexion of his family, who, he believed, had procured it some years before, from the library of a Roman Catholic family of the name of Perkins, of Upton Court, Berkshire, one member of which had married Arabella Farmer, the heroine of ' The Rape of the Lock.'

" Those particulars were, as kindly as promptly, communicated to me by Mr. Moore, with whom I was not personally acquainted ; and he urged Mr. Parry also to write to me on the subject ; but that gentleman was prevented from doing so by a

but in the main agrees with that quoted from
the *Notes and Emendations*; and it will be observed that neither of these narratives, published

---

serious fall, which confined him to his bed. Being, of course,
much interested in the question, I soon afterwards took an
opportunity of introducing myself to Mr. Moore, who, satisfied
that Mr. Parry had formerly been the proprietor of my copy of
the folio 1632, advised me to call upon that gentleman at his
house, Hill Road, St. John's Wood, assuring me that he would
be glad to give me all the information in his power.

"I was, I think, the first person whom Mr. Parry saw after
his accident ; and in a long interview he repeated to me the
statement which he had previously made to Mr. Moore, respecting the gift of Mr. Gray half a century ago, and his conviction
of the identity of the volume. He could not prove the fact, but
he had always understood and believed, that Mr. Gray had
become possessed of it on the dispersion of the library of the
Perkins family at Upton Court, and that it had been in his
hands some years before the conclusion of the last century.
Mr. Parry had himself had the curiosity to visit Upton Court
about 1803 or 1804 ; when a Roman Catholic priest, not less
than 80 years old, showed him the library and the then empty
shelves, from which the books had been removed.

" On referring subsequently to the ' Magna Britannia ' of
Lysons, under the head of ' Berkshire,' I found various parti-
culars regarding the Perkins family at Upton Court, between
1635 and 1738 ; but I did not meet with any mention of Thomas
Perkins, whose name, it will be remembered, is on the cover of
the folio 1632, in question. The name of the distinguished
actor of the reigns of James the First and Charles the First, was
Richard Perkins ; and Ashmole's Collections, according to
Lysons, speak of a Richard Perkins as the husband of Lady
Mervin, of Upton Court. It is just possible that this Richard

at the time when the occurrence actually took place, countenance in the slightest degree Mr. Collier's subsequent belief that he had exhibited the volume itself to the examination of Mr. Parry.

Perkins was the actor; for, although the 'Historia Histrionica' tells us that he was buried at Clerkenwell, that authority is by no means final: just before it notices the death of Perkins, it speaks of Lowin as having expired in great poverty at Brentford, when we know that this 'player' (so designated in the register) was buried at St. Clement Danes, Strand, on the 24th of August, 1653. However, it is a mere speculation that the Richard Perkins who married Lady Mervin may have been the actor, and I am not yet in possession of any other dates or circumstances to guide me.

"Having put in writing the particulars with which Mr. Parry had so unreservedly favoured me, I took the liberty of forwarding them to Mr. Moore; and he returned the manuscript with his full approbation as regarded what had originally passed between himself and Mr. Parry. After it was in type, I again waited upon Mr. Parry, only three days ago, in order that I might read the proof to him, and introduce such additions and corrections as he wished to be made. They were few, but not unimportant; and among them was the fact (confirming the probability that Mr. Gray had obtained this copy of the folio 1632, from the Perkins library) that Mr. Gray resided at Newbury, not far from Upton Court—a circumstance which Mr. Parry had previously omitted. The connecting link between the book and this library is, therefore, not complete; and we have still to ascertain, if we can, who was Thomas Perkins, and by whom the notes and emendations were introduced into the folio 1632. A Francis Perkins died at Upton Court in 1635, and he may have been the first purchaser and owner of this second folio of the works of Shakespeare. ["At

Here the *extrinsic* evidences against the authenticity of the corrected folio of 1632 may be brought to a close : nor is it to be forgotten that the *internal* proofs of its spurious character are no less powerful, and have long since been independently urged against it by Singer, Dyce, Knight, Staunton, Halliwell, Ingleby, Grant White, and the whole phalanx of Shaksperian Commentators. That any one, using due consideration, can still maintain the authority of the volume, seems not possible.

"At all events, however, it is certain that this very volume was for many years in the possession of Mr. Parry (how he lost it he knows not), who obtained it from his connexion, Mr. George Gray, of Newbury. Mr. Parry was well acquainted with the fact that various leaves were wanting; and he so perfectly recollects its state and condition, the frequent erasures of passages, as well as the handwriting of the numerous marginal and other corrections, that when I asked him, just before I wished him good morning, whether he had any doubt on the point of his previous ownership, he answered me most emphatically in these words—'I have no more doubt about it, than that you are sitting there.'

"J. PAYNE COLLIER.

" *Maidenhead, May* 28."

"P.S.—I ought not to omit the expression of my warmest acknowledgments to both Mr. Moore and Mr. Parry, for the zealous and ready assistance which they have afforded me. I hope that if any of the readers of the *Athenæum* are in possession of information that may tend to the further elucidation of the subject, they will communicate it with equal alacrity."

But the facts I am now about to advert to are far graver than the question of the authenticity of that or any other particular volume. They have reference to a *series* of systematic forgeries which have been perpetrated, apparently within the last half century, and are in connection generally with the history of Shakspere and Shaksperian literature, although other subjects have occasionally been introduced.

The first instance I shall bring forward, as being more nearly related than any other to the question of the annotated edition of 1632, is that of Lord Ellesmere's first edition of Shakspere's Plays, 1623. This folio his Lordship submitted to my scrutiny, subsequently to the publication in *The Times* of my remarks on the folio belonging to the Duke of Devonshire. Like it, Lord Ellesmere's folio has also received marginal annotations. In both instances the corrections have been made first in pencil and afterwards in ink, the mode of obliteration is characteristic and similar, and on examination I recognise *the same hand-writing in both.*

Beyond the fact that Lord Ellesmere's volume was supposed to be the finest copy of the first folio in existence, little seems to have been known

about it, until the year 1842, when the late Lord
Ellesmere, then Lord Francis Egerton, lent the
volume to Mr. Collier.   How long it remained in
that gentleman's custody I am not aware. But subsequently, Mr. Collier published a letter addressed
by him to the Rev. Joseph Hunter, in which he
mentions the loan of the volume, and states that
he has discovered in its pages some important marginal emendations, examples of which he proceeds
to cite.   The alterations in this first folio are
not numerous, but they are frequently identical
with those afterwards discovered by Mr. Collier
in the folio of 1632; the identity in one or
two instances being strikingly significant.   Prior
to their discovery by Mr. Collier, it does not
seem, so far as I can learn, that any alterations
were known to exist on the margins at all.   He
is certainly wrong in attributing them to the time
of the Commonwealth ; they are not only modern,
but, decidedly, *by the same hand* as those in
his more famous copy of the second edition.
I subjoin Mr. Collier's account of the discovery ;
also a list of the whole of the corrections found in
the edition of 1623, in which I have been careful
to distinguish such as likewise occur in the
" Folio " 1632.

"Reasons for a New Edition of Shakespeare's Works. 1842.
By Mr. John Payne Collier, p. 13."

" Lord Francis Egerton was also kind enough to add
to the obligation, by lending me his folios of 1623
and 1632; the first being more than ordinarily interesting on account of certain early manuscript corrections in
a few of the plays, which will put an end to doubts on
some passages of the original text, and will most satisfactorily illustrate and explain others not hitherto well understood.   *   *   *   These corrections in the
margin of the printed portion of the folio, are probably
as old as the reign of Charles I.   Whether they were
merely conjectural, or were made from original MSS. of
the plays to which the individual might have had access,
it is not perhaps possible to ascertain; it has been stated,
these verbal, and sometimes literal, annotations, are only
found in a few of the plays in the commencement of the
volume, and from what follows, it will be a matter of
deep regret that the corrector of the text carried his
labours no further."

L

Manuscript Corrections in the Bridgewater folio, 1623.

Printed Text of Folio 1623.	*MS. Corrections.*

As You Like It, p. 191, c. 2.

[*Wearing*] thy hearer in thy mistris praise

[Wearying] but afterwards obliterated. This is the printed reading in 1632.

Do., p. 204, c. 1.

I will ore-run thee with polic[*e*]

[y] obliterated. The printed reading of 1632.

All's Well, p. 234, c. 1.

The mistrie of yon lo[*u*]elinesse, and finded

[n]   [v] in ed. 1632.

Do., p. 236, c. 1.

Where hope is coldest, and despair most [*shifts*]

[ffits] fits 1632.

Measure for Measure, p. 63, col. 2.

(The needful bits and curbes to headstrong [*weedes*])

[steedes]
The same cor. has been made in the folio 1632, but afterwards obliterated.

Do., p. 70, c. 1.

Owe, and succeed [*thy*] weaknesse

[this] *with a trace of pencil.* The same cor. in the folio of 1632.

Love's Labour Lost, p. 133, c. 1.

Disfigure not his [*Shop.*]

[shape] slop 1632.

As You Like It, p. 189, c. 2.

After my flight: now goe [*in we*] content

[we in] *we in* printed in 1632.

Do., p. 190, c. 2.

ᴀ Why, what's the matter?

[ORL.] in print in 1632.

All's Well, &c., p. 240, c. 1.

[*A*]nd ere I do begin

[E] The same correction is made in folio 1632.

Do., &c., p. 125. c. 1.

LAF. You begge more than ᴀ word then

[a] with a trace of pencil underneath. [one] 1632, but blotted, a pencil distinct underneath the ink.

Printed Text of Folio 1623.	*MS. Corrections.*
All's Well, &c., p. 252, c. 2.	
KING. I wonder, Sir, [*Sir,*]	[for]
I wonder, [*Sir,*] wives are such monsters to you	[since] in ed. 1632, but almost wholly obliterated.
Winter's Tale, p. 279, c. 1.	
Of my Boyes face, m[*e*] thoughts I did me requoyle	[y] y 1632
Do., p. 280, c. 1.	
My Wife's a Ho[*l*]y-Horse	[b] b 1632
Do., p. 285, c. 2.	
So sure as th[*is*] Beard's gray	[y] your 1632
Do., p. 294, c. 1.	
And hand͜ ed love, as you do ; I was wont	[l] pencil traceable. [l] 1632.
Do., p. 299, c. 1.	
Above a better, gone ; so must thy gra[*v*]e	[c] pencil distinct.
Do., p. 299, c. 2.	
Give you all greetings, that a king (a[*t*] friend)	[s] *as* printed in 1632.

But besides the marginal corrections in Lord Ellesmere's folio, Mr. Collier likewise discovered in the library of Bridgewater House, a series of remarkable documents of the highest interest, supposing them genuine, in regard to the life of Shakspere. The particulars of the discovery were made public in a letter addressed to Mr. George Amyot in the year 1835. In this letter Mr. Collier dwells at considerable length upon the importance of the documents in question, but does not hint at anything in the appearance of the handwriting calculated to throw doubts upon their genuineness; while the particulars stated respecting their being contained in bundles of manuscript, probably unopened since the days of Chancellor Ellesmere, would tell strongly in their favour. Some of these particulars I transcribe from Mr. Collier's letter.

However assuring and satisfactory the particulars respecting the discovery of these MSS. as thus stated by Mr. Collier, the contents of the documents themselves, when carefully considered, were of a nature not merely to raise suspicion, but to shake belief in them altogether, as I shall presently show.

In addition to this it was understood that two skilled palæographists, the Rev. Joseph Hunter, and Mr. Black (both of the Public Record Office), having had an opportunity of examining the originals, had privately expressed an opinion adverse to their pretensions as authentic documents, judging from the handwriting. But to Mr. Halliwell is the real merit due of having stated distinctly the whole case against these remarkable documents. This he did in a pamphlet printed "for private circulation only," in 1853, the pamphlet being accompanied by a *fac-simile* of one of the documents in question. His argument is so forcible, that I prefer to quote his own words.

" When I came to make a personal inspection of these interesting papers, facilities for which were kindly granted by their noble owner, grave doubts were at once created as to their authenticity. The most important of all, the certificate from the players of the Blackfriars' Theatre to the Privy Council in 1589, instead of being either an original or a contemporary copy, is evidently at best merely a late transcript, if it be not altogether a recent fabrication. The question naturally arises, for what purpose could a document of this description have been copied in the seventeenth century, presuming it to belong to so early a period ? It is comparatively of recent times that the slightest literary interest has been taken in the history of our early theatres, or even in the biography of Shakespeare ; and, unless it was apparent that papers of this kind were transcribed for some legal or other special purpose, there should be great hesitation in accepting the evidence of any other but contemporary authority. The suspicious appearance of this certificate is of itself sufficient to justify great difficulties in its reception; but the doubt thus induced as to the integrity of the collection was considerably increased by an examination of a paper in the same volume purporting to be a warrant appointing Daborne, Shakespeare, Field, and Kirkham, instructors of the children of the Queen's Revels, which unquestionably appears to be a modern forgery. This document is styled by Mr. Collier, " a draft either for a Patent or a Privy Seal." It is not a draft, for the lines are written bookwise, and it is also dated; neither is it a copy of a patent, as appears from the direction, " Right trustie & well-beloved;" but, if genuine, it must be considered an abridged transcript of a warrant, under the sign-manual and signet, for a patent to be issued. Now if it be shewn that the letters patent to " Daborne & others " were granted on the same day on which Lord Ellesmere's paper is dated, and, if it be further proved that the contents of the latter are altogether inconsistent with the circumstances detailed in the real patent, it will, I think, be conceded that no genuine draft or transcript of the nature of that printed by Mr. Collier, can possibly exist.

" It appears that the following note occurs in an entry-book of patents that passed the Great Seal while it was in the hands of Lord Ellesmere, in 7 James I.: — " A Warrant for Robert Daborne and others, the Queene's Servants, to bring up and practice children in places by

the name of the Children of the Queen's Revells, for the
pleasure of her Majestie, 4° Januarii, anno septimo
Jacobi." This entry may have suggested the fabrication, the date of the questionable MS. corresponding
with that here given ; though it is capable of proof that
if it were authentic, it must have been dated previously,
for the books of the Signet Office show that the authority for Daborne's warrant was obtained by the influence
of Sir Thomas Munson in the previous December, and
they also inform us that it was granted "to Robert
Daborne, and other Servauntes to the Queen, from time
to time, to provide and bring up a convenient number
of children to practize in the quality of playing, by the
name of the Children of the Revells to the Queene, *in
the White Fryers, London,* or any other convenient place
where he shall thinke fit." The enrolment of the instrument, which was issued in the form of letters patent
under the Great Seal, recites, " Whereas the Queen, our
dearest wyfe, hathe for hir pleasure and recreacion,
when shee shall thinke it fitt to have any playes or
shewes, appoynted hir servantes Robert Daborne, Phil-
lipe Rosseter, John Tarbock, Richard Jones, and Robert Browne, to provide and bring upp a convenient
nomber of Children, whoe shalbe called Children of hir
Revelles, Know yee that wee have appoynted and
authorised, and by theis presentes do authorize and
appoynte the saide Robert Daborne, &c. from tyme to
tyme, to provide, keepe and bring upp a convenient
nomber of children, and them to practice and exercise
in the quality of playing, by the name of Children of

the Revells to the Queene, within the White Fryers in the suburbs of our Citty of London, or in any other convenyent place where they shall thinke fitt for that purpose." This patent is dated January 4th, 7 Jac. I., 1609-10, so that any draft, or projected warrant, exhibiting other names than the above, could not possibly have had this exact date. It will be observed that the names, with the exception of that of Daborne, are entirely different in the two documents, and this company of children was to play at the Whitefriars, not at the Blackfriars. The fabricator seems to have relied on the supposition that the entry relative to Daborne and others referred to the latter theatre ; and consequently inserted the name of Edward Kirkham, who is known to have been one of the instructors of the children of the Revels at the Blackfriars in the year 1604. There is, in fact, no reasonable supposition on which the Ellesmere paper can be regarded as authentic. Had no date been attached to it, it might have been said that the whole related merely to some contemplated arrangement which was afterwards altered ; although even in that case, the form of the copy would alone have been a serious reason against its reception. In its present state, it is clearly impossible to reconcile it with the contents of the enrolment just quoted. Fortunately for the interests of truth, indications of forgery are detected in trifling circumstances, that are almost invariably neglected by the inventor, however ingeniously the deception be contrived. Were it not for this, the search for historical truth would yield results sufficiently uncertain to deter the most enthusiastic enquirer from pursuing the investigation.

"The remaining Shakesperian MSS. in the possession of the Earl of Ellesmere, consist of a letter of Daniel the poet, mentioning the great dramatist as a candidate for the Mastership of the Queen's Revels; accounts in which a performance of *Othello* is stated to have taken place in the year 1602; a remarkable paper detailing the value of the shares held by Shakespeare and others in the Blackfriars Theatre; and the presumed early copy of a letter signed "H. S.," supposed to have been written by Lord Southampton, and containing singular notices of Burbage and Shakespeare. The first two of them I have not seen, the volume including only a recent transcript of Daniel's letter; but the other two, which have been carefully inspected, present an appearance by no means satisfactory. Although the caligraphy is of a highly skilful character, and, judging solely from a fac-simile of the letter, I should certainly have accepted it as genuine, yet an examination of the original leads to a different judgment; the paper and ink not appearing to belong to so early a date. It is a suspicious circumstance that both these documents are written in an unusually large character on folio leaves of paper, by *the same hand*, and are evidently not contemporaneous copies. Again may the question be asked, Why should transcripts of such papers have been made after the period to which the originals are supposed to refer? It is also curious that copies only of these important records should be preserved; and the whole

M

matter is surrounded by the gravest suspicions and difficulties.

"Only one record-reader, as far as I know, viz., the Rev. Joseph Hunter, has made a personal examination of these MSS. He has not yet expressed any opinion publicly, but I have reason to think that his views on the subject coincide with my own. It is clearly Mr. Collier's duty, as a lover of truth, to have the originals carefully scrutinized by the best judges of the day."

On the 17th of November, 1859, I had an opportunity of carefully examining these Bridgewater MSS. for myself, in company with Sir Frederic Madden and Dr. Kingsley. How it was Mr. Collier deceived himself as to their real character I will not attempt to speculate. With one exception, which manifests some dexterity of execution, these documents display their spurious character at a glance; whilst two of the number (the Daborne warrant and Daniel's letter), are such manifest forgeries, that it seems incredible how they could have cheated Mr. Collier's observation, even under the circumstances of excitement described by him as consequent upon their discovery.*

---

* "When first I obtained permission to look through the Bridgewater MSS. in detail, I conjectured that it would be nearly impossible to turn over so many state papers and such a bulk of correspondence, private and official, without meeting with

Annexed is a fac-simile of the spurious Daborne warrant. Independently of every other evidence of its fictitious character, the form alone in which it is drawn, is sufficient to make one

---

something illustrative of the subject to which I have devoted so many years ; but I certainly never anticipated being so fortunate as to obtain particulars so new, curious, and important, regarding a poet who, above all others, ancient or modern, native or foreign, has been the object of admiration. When I took up the copy of Lord Southampton's letter and glanced over it hastily, I could scarcely believe my eyes to see such names as Shakespeare and Burbage in connection in a manuscript of the time. There was a remarkable coincidence also in the discovery, for it happened on the anniversary of Shakespeare's birth and death. I will not attempt to describe my joy and surprise, and I can only liken it to the unexpected gratification I experienced two or three years ago, when I turned out, from some ancient depositories of the Duke of Devonshire, the original designs of Inigo Jones, not only for the scenery, but for the dresses and characters of the different masques by Ben Jonson, Campion, Townsend, &c., presented at Court in the reigns of our first James and Charles. The sketches were sometimes accompanied by explanations in the handwriting of the great artist, a few of which incidentally illustrate Shakespeare, who, however, was never employed for any of these royal entertainments. Annexed to one of the drawings was the following written description, from whence we learn how the actor of the part of Falstaff was usually habited in the time of Shakespeare.

" ' Like a Sir Jon Falstaff: in a roabe of russet, quite low, with a great belley, like a swolen man, long moustacheos, the sheows [shoes] shorte, and out of them great toes like naked feete : buskins to sheaw a great swolen leg. A cupp coming

look upon it with the greatest doubt, the style of
the Sovereign being placed after the opening
words of the body of the warrant; a position in-
conceivable in any authentic instrument. A
minute of the genuine document, which differs
wholly from the above, was discovered by Mr.
Halliwell, in an entry-book of Patents that
passed the Great Seal while it was in the hands
of Lord Ellesmere in 7 James I;* and which is
entirely confirmed by an entry made by the Chancellor's riding-clerk in the "Book of Warrants
which have passed the Great Seal," amongst the
Bridgewater MSS.; thus affording another proof
of the spurious nature of the warrant published
by Mr. Collier.

Much as these five documents† vary in manner
and style of execution, no one, I think, who

---

fourth like a beake—a great head and balde, and a little cap
alla Venetiane greay—a rodd and a scroule of parchment.'"—
*New Facts regarding the Life of Shakespeare, in a Letter to Thomas
Amyot, from J. Payne Collier,* 1835.

It is somewhat remarkable that neither this drawing nor
the description of Falstaff are to be found in the Shakspere
Society's volume, edited by J. R. Planché, Esq., from the Duke
of Devonshire's Library. The language of the "description"
is, to say the least, suspicious.—[H.]

* See Observations on the Shaksperian Forgeries, by James
O. Halliwell, Esq., 1853, p. 5.

† These documents are given in Appendix I.

examines them carefully (tracing through the whole of them similarities in the forms of certain letters, and even identity of mistakes), can doubt but that they are all the work of one pen. Nor can I too pointedly reiterate my belief *that the whole of the forgeries treated of in this volume have been executed by one hand.* The same exaggerations, the same blunders, and even the same excellencies in performance being observable in Mr. Collier's corrected folio, 1632, in Lord Ellesmere's folio, 1623, in the Bridgewater Manuscripts under discussion, and in the Dulwich forgeries, and the document in the State Paper Office described further on. In regard to the two former, indeed, this fact is pretty well indicated, not only by the handwriting itself, but by the similar use of pencil marks to direct the ink corrections, and by a precisely similar mode of erasure.

I pass from the Bridgewater Papers to an examination of the manuscripts in Dulwich College; and I commence by stating certain facts relative to the *misinterpretation* of a letter to which I have already alluded in the Preface, and where the question is not of a spurious document, but of a *mis-read* copy of one that is genuine.

In 1841 Mr. Collier edited for the Shakspere

Society a volume, entitled " Memoirs of Edward
Alleyn." Amongst the Documents published by
Mr. Collier in this volume is one correctly stated
to be an original letter from Mrs. Alleyn, wife of
the founder of Dulwich College, and addressed to
her husband. The letter in itself is interesting;
but the point upon which Mr. Collier mainly
insists, as constituting its peculiar value, is a
paragraph he prints as contained in it, relative to
" Mr. Shakespeare of the Globe," and from which
he proceeds to draw various deductions. On
collating this letter with the original, it appears
to have been entirely misread by Mr. Collier, *as
there is not the smallest trace of authority for
any allusion to Shakspere, or to any of the
words concerning him found there by Mr. Collier,
and printed by him as forming part of the
original document.* I subjoin the whole of
Mr. Collier's remarks and comments upon the
letter, because his description of the physical
appearance of its lower margin defaced by damp,
and the passage in the letter at which the leaf
turns over, are sufficient to identify the actual
paper which he had before him, proving it to
be the same as I have myself since examined,
and not, as might possibly be suggested, another

Facsimile of a portion of a letter of Mrs Allayn, preserved at Dulwich College.

F. G. Netherclift facsim.lith. 17 Well. St. Covent.Gdn.

copy in which the contents were altered; and, in addition, because his account of the difficulties attendant on deciphering it, lead one to the conclusion that he had himself minutely examined it.

" Of this date we have a very interesting letter from Mrs. Alleyn to her husband, written and subscribed by the person ordinarily employed : it is remarkable, because it contains a mention of Shakespeare, who is spoken of as ' of the Globe ;' and though it throws no new light upon our great dramatist's character, excepting as it shows that he was on good terms with Alleyn's family, any document containing merely his name must be considered valuable. The paper on which the letter was written is in a most decayed state, especially at the bottom, where it breaks and drops away in dust and fragments at the slightest touch. The notice of Shakespeare is near the commencement of a postscript on the lower part of the page, where the paper is most rotten, and several deficiencies occur, which it is impossible to supply : all that remains is extremely difficult to be deciphered.* We will insert it, and defer further remarks until afterwards, only premising that the address

---

* This description, both as to the decayed state of the paper, as well as to the difficulty of deciphering the handwriting, seems to me a very exaggerated one. On the latter point, the accompanying fac-simile will enable the reader to form an independent judgment.—[H.]

has completely disappeared, so that we cannot tell where Alleyn was at the time ; nor, indeed, excepting from internal evidence, can we decide that it was sent to him. Upon this point, however, there can be no doubt."— *Memoirs of Alleyn*, ed. Collier, p. 62.

I contrast on opposite pages two versions of this document; the first is a copy made by myself, and containing a true reading of the original, the second is that published by Mr. Collier in the *Memoirs of Alleyn*, p. 62. I have broken the lines, both in my version of the document and in that of Mr. Collier, in exact accordance with the written document, so that the reader may see at a glance the average number of words contained in a line, and be thereby enabled to judge for himself of the actual impossibility of the paragraph in question having ever been contained in the original document where Mr. Collier avers that he found it. At the same time it will be observed that portions of three damaged lines are still legible, which are incompatible with the *Shakspere paragraph*, and in regard to which Mr. Collier is wholly silent. I need not remark that a case of misreading, and miscopying, however gross, is not to be confounded with the innumerable forgeries, (by whomsoever perpetrated,) which it is the object of this volume to bring to light; but it is for the literary world to estimate the magnitude and the character of the wrong done to literature by announcements of such a nature and of so deliberate a kind.

The *thirty-two* minor blunders, literal and verbal, which occur in Mr. Collier's professedly *verbatim* and *literatim* copy of this letter of Mrs. Alleyn, are of less importance, although not undeserving of reprehension. The Rev. A. Dyce, in his "Strictures on Mr. Collier's New Edition of Shakespeare, 1858," has published a series of alleged misstatements and inaccuracies committed by Mr. Collier, which would be incredible, were they not vouched for by the name of a scholar of Mr. Dyce's unimpeachable truth and accuracy.

N

*Copy of Mrs. Alleyn's Letter, preserved at Dulwich College,
verbatim, literatim, and line for line.*

JHESUS.

My intyre and welbeloved sweete harte still it joyes me and longe I
pray god maye I joye to heare of your healthe and welfare as you of ours.
Allmighty God be thancked my owne selfe your selfe and my mother and
whole house are in good healthe and about us the sycknes doth cease
and likely more and more by godes healpe to cease. All the companyes
be come hoame and well for ought we knowe, but that Browne of
the Boares head is dead and dyed very pore. He went not into the
owne   countrye at all, and all of your ∧ company ar well at theyr owne houses.
My father is at the corte, but wheare the court ys I know not.
I am of your owne mynde that it is needles to meete my fathere
at Basynge, the Incertayntye beinge as it ys, I commend your
discreation. It were a sore journey to loase your labour besyd expenses
and change of ayre might hurte you, therfore you are resolved upon
the best course. For your cominge hoame I am not to advyse you,
neither will I ; use your owne discreation, yet I longe and am very
desyrous to see you, and my poore and symple opinion is, yf it shall please
you, you maye safely come hoame. Heare is none now sycke neare
us : yet let it not be as I wyll but at your owne best lykynge. I am
glad to heare you take delight in hauckinge and thoughe you
have   ∧worne your appayrell to rags, the best ys you knowe
wheare to have better, and as wellcome to me shall you be with
your rags as yf you were in cloathe of gold or velvet. Trye
and see. I have payd fyfty shillings for your rent for the warfe,
not in towne   the Lordes rent. Mr. Woodward, my Lordes bayly was ∧ but poynted
his deputy who receaved all the rentes. I had witnesses with
me at the payment of the money and have his quittance, but
the quyttance cost me a groat, they sayd it was the baylives
fee. You know best whether you were wont to paye it : yf not,
they made a symple woman of me. You shall receave a letter
from the Joyner hym selfe and a prynted bill, and so with my

Mrs. Alleyn's Letter, as printed in the "Memoirs of Alleyn," *p.* 62, *ed. J. P. Collier*, 1841.

"JHESUS.

" My intyre and welbeloved sweete harte, still it joyes me and longe, I
pray god, may I joye to heare of your healthe and welfare, *as of* ours.
Allmighty god be *thanked*, my *own* selfe, your selfe and my mother, and
whole house are in good healthe, and about us the sycknes dothe cease
and likely more and more by *gods* healpe to cease. All the companyes
be come *home* and well for ought we knowe, but that Browne of
the Boares head is dead, and dyed very pore. He went not into the
countrye at all, and all of your owne company ar well at *there* owne houses.
My father is at the corte, but wheare the *corte* ys I know not.
I am of your owne mynde, that it is needles to meete my *father*
at Basynge : the *entertaynment* beinge as it *is*, I *comend* your
discreation. It *weare* a sore journey to loase your labour, *besyde* expenses,
and change of ayre *mighte* hurte you ; therfore you are resolved upon
the best course. For your cominge hoame I am not to advyse you,
neither will I : use your owne discreation, yet I longe and am very
desyrous to see you ; and my poore and *simple* opinion is, yf it shall please
you, you maye safely come hoame. Heare is none now sycke neare
us ; yet let it not be as I wyll, but at your owne best lykynge. I am
glad to heare you take delight in hauckinge, and thoughe you
have worne your appayrell to rags, the best ys you knowe
where to have better, and as wellcome to me shall you be with
your rags, as yf you were in cloathe of gold or velvet. Trye
and see. I have payd fyfty shillings for your rent for the warfe,
the Lordes rent. Mr. Woodward, my Lordes bayly, was not in towne but poynted
his deputy who receaved all the rentes. I had witnesses with
me at the payment of the money, and have his quittance, but
the quyttance cost me a groat : they sayd it was the baylives
fee. You *knowe* best whether you were wont to paye it ; yf not,
they made a symple woman of me. You shall receave a letter
from the Joyner hym selfe, and a prynted bill ; and so with my

*

Mrs. Alleyn's Letter—continued.

humble and harty comendations to your owne selfe, Mr. Chaloners
and his wyfe, with thanckes for your kynde usage, with my good
mothers kyndest commendations with the rest of your houshould
God . . . dle is well but can not speake, I ende prayenge allmighty_A
his still to blesse us for _A mercyes sake, and so sweete harte
once more farwell till we meete, which I hope shall not
be longe. This xxth of October 1603.

Aboute a weeke agoe there [cam]e a youthe who said he was
Mr. Frauncis Chalo[ner]s man . . . . ld have borrow[e]d x' to
bought have _A things for [h]is Mr. . . . . t hym
Cominge without . . . token . . . . d
I would have . . . .
& I bene su . . . .
and inquire after the fellow and said he had lent hym a horse. I
us feare me he gulled hym, thoughe he gulled not _A. The youthe
what was a prety youthe and hansom in appayrell, we know not _A became
of hym. Mr. Bromffeild commendes hym: he was heare yesterdaye. Nicke
and Jeames be well, and commend them, so dothe Mr. Cooke and his weife
in the kyndest sorte, and so once more in the hartiest manner
farwelle

Your faithfull and lovinge weife

JOANE ALLEYNE.

Mrs. Alleyn's Letter (ed. J. P. Collier)—continued.

humble and harty comendations to your owne selfe, Mr. Chaloners
and his wyfe, with *thankes* for your kynde usage, with my good
mothers kyndest *comendations* with the rest of your *househould*
*   *   *he* is well but can not speake, I ende *prayinge* allmighty god
to blesse *you* for his mercyes sake, and so sweete harte
*   *   *noe more. Farwell* till we meete, which I hope shall not
be longe.   This xxth of October 1603.

   " Aboute a weeke a goe there came a youthe who said he was
Mr. Frauncis Chaloner who would have borrowed x^li to
have bought things for   *   *   *   and said he was known
unto you, and Mr. Shakespeare of the globe, who came
*   *   *   said he knewe hym not, only he herde of hym that he was
a roge   *   *   *   so he was glade we did not lend him
the monney   *   *   *   Richard Johnes [went] to seeke
and inquire after the fellow, and said he had lent hym a horse.   I
feare me he gulled hym, thoughe he gulled not us.   The youthe
was a prety youthe, and hansom in appayrell : we *knowe* not what became
of hym.   Mr. *Benfield* commendes hym ; he was heare yesterdaye.   Nicke
and Jeames be well, and *comend* them : so *doth* Mr. Cooke and his *wiefe*
in the kyndest sorte, and so once more in the hartiest manner
farwell.

                     " Your faithfull and lovinge *wiefe,*
                                   " JOANE ALLEYNE."

Dulwich College, however, is not without its forgeries. Of these I shall cite three examples, all of them first printed by Mr. Collier, in the same volume as that from which the inaccurate copy of Mrs. Alleyn's letter is already quoted, and all of them (as he states in the body of that work) discovered by him.

The first of these which I shall notice is a letter of John Marston, printed in the *Memoirs of Alleyn*, p. 154, and which will be found in the Appendix to this volume.

In its general aspect the writing of this letter certainly resembles Marston's genuine hand, and has no doubt been executed by some one to whom that hand was familiar; but I soon noticed the existence of numerous modern pencil-marks underlying the ink, and on looking closely into the document, detected that *the whole of the letter had been first traced out in pencil, after the same fashion as the pencilling in the annotated folio of Shakspere's Plays*, 1632; and I may here remark that the existence of this system of pencilling in this letter at Dulwich College, as well as in Mr. Collier's and Lord Ellesmere's folios, seems of much importance in tracing these various fictitious documents up to one source, although other forgeries exist in the same libraries in which pencil-marks cannot be discovered, but which nevertheless there is reason for believing were perpetrated by the same hand. Of such forgeries I proceed to mention two : both of them in the library at Dulwich, both relating to Shakspere, and both, as before said, first published in the *Memoirs of Alleyn*, (p. 13.)

The first of these, the verses commencing,—

"Sweet Nedde, nowe wynne an other wager,"

is a forgery from beginning to end, although executed with singular dexterity. In the second the document itself is genuine, and is noticed in his "Inquiry" by Malone, but the "List of Players" added to it, in which Shakspere's name occurs, is a modern addition. Mr. Collier was the first to notice and publish this "List of Players;" but although he draws attention to the circumstance that Malone, while mentioning the letter, is altogether silent as to the remarkable "List" appended to it, he does not appear to regard this as a ground for suspecting the authenticity of the List, but seems to think that a satisfactory explanation may be found by supposing that Malone had "reserved" it for his Life of Shakspere: the true explanation, doubtless, being, that when Malone examined the document, the "List" in question was not there,

but has been added since his time. Any one
who will compare the character of the hand in
which the "List" is written, with the letter
signed H. S. in the Bridgewater library, will
probably arrive at the conclusion I have done,
that they are by the same hand.

But of the various documents which I believe
to be spurious, the most remarkable is the following :—

To the right honorable the Ll of her Maties most
honorable priuie Counsell

The humble petition of Thomas Pope Richard Burbadge John Hemings Augustine Phillips Willm Shakespeare Willm Kempe Willm Slye Nicholas Tooley and
others seruauntes to the right honorable the L. Cham-
berlaine to her Matie—Sheweth most humbly that yor
petitioners are owners and players of the priuate
house or theater in the precinct and libertie of the
Blackfriers wch hath beene for manie yeares vsed and
occupied for the playing of tragedies commedies his-
tories enterludes and playes. That the same by reason
of having beene soe long built hath falne into great decaye
and that besides the reparation thereof it hath beene
found necessarie to make the same more conuenient for
the entertainement of auditories comming thereto
That to this end yor petitioners haue all and eche of them
putt down sommes of money according to their shares in

the saide theater and wch they haue iustly and honestlie
gained by the exercise of their qualitie of Stage players
but that certaine persons (some of them of honour)
inhabitantes of the precinct and libertie of the Black-
friers haue as yor petitioners are enfourmed besought yor
honorable Lps not to permitt the saide priuate house anie
longer to remaine open but hereafter to be shutt vpp
and closed to the manifest and great iniurie of yor petitioners who haue no other meanes whereby to mainteine
their wiues and families but by the exersise of their
qualitie as they haue heretofore done.   Furthermore
that in the summer season yor petitioners are able to
playe at their newe built house on the Bankside callde
the Globe but that in the winter they are compelled to
come to the Blackfriers and if yor honorable Lps give
consent vnto that wch is prayde against yor petitioners
they will not onely while the winter endureth loose the
meanes whereby they nowe support them selues and
their families but be vnable to practise them selues in
anie playes or enterluds when calde vpon to performe
for the recreation and solace of her Matie and her
honorable Court as they haue beene hertofore accustomed.
The humble prayer of yor petitioners therefore is that
yor hon^{ble} Lps will graunt permission to finishe the repa-
rations and alterations they haue begunne and as yor
petitioners haue hitherto beene well ordred in their
behauiour and iust in their dealinges that yor honorable
Lps will not inhibit them from acting at their aboue
named priuate house in the precinct and libertie of the
Blackfriers and yor petitioners as in dutie most bounden

O

will euer praye for the encreasing honour and happinesse of your honorable Lps.*

Up to this point, the value of any addition, however slight, to the knowledge we possess regarding Shakspere's history, has alone given importance to the inquiry whether the documents from which such additional facts were taken, were genuine, as they professed to be. But the document above printed, claims, at the present moment, the dignity and credit of a Public Record. It is preserved in Her Majesty's State Paper Office, bears upon it the official stamp of that office, and forms one of a collection of public papers of undoubted genuineness. Yet there can be little question that it belongs to the same set of *forgeries* as those already investigated : that by some means, yet to be traced, it has been surreptitiously introduced among the Records where it is now found ; and in the course of official routine has received with the rest the stamp of authenticity.

A fac-simile of it is given by Mr. Halliwell, in his folio Shakspere, 1853, (vol. i. p. 137), who states that it was discovered by Mr. Collier in the State Paper Office ; and Mr. Collier prints it in

---

* Document preserved in H.M.'s State Paper Office, Domestic Series,—Elizabeth, 1596, Bundle 222.

his Annals of the Stage (1831), with the following notice : — " This remarkable paper has, perhaps, never seen the light from the moment it was presented, until it was very recently discovered. It is seven years anterior to the date of any other authentic record which contains the name of our great dramatist."*

---

* The following is the entire passage in which Mr. Collier states the discovery of the record. " The Blackfriars Theatre, built in 1576, seems, after the lapse of twenty years, to have required extensive repairs, if, indeed, it were not at the end of that period entirely rebuilt. This undertaking, in 1596, seems to have alarmed some of the inhabitants of the Liberty; and not a few of them, 'some of honour,' petitioned the Privy Council, in order that the players might not be allowed to complete it, and that their further performances in that precinct might be prevented. A copy of the document containing this request, is preserved in the State Paper Office, and to it is appended a much more curious paper—a counter petition by the Lord Chamberlain's players, entreating that they might be permitted to continue their work upon the theatre, in order to render it more commodious, and that their performances there might not be interrupted. It does not appear to be the original, but a copy without the signatures, and it contains at the commencement, an enumeration of the principal actors who were parties to it. They occur in the following order, and it will be instantly remarked, not only that the name of Shakespeare is found among them, but that he comes fifth in the enumeration :—

Thomas Pope,
Richard Burbage,
John Hemings,

This petition bears no date, and is written on half a sheet of foolscap paper, without water-mark, and which, from the appearance of the edges, I should think had probably once formed the fly-leaf of some folio volume. A supposed date of 1596 has been placed upon it in pencil by one of the gentlemen in the State Paper Office. Its execution is very neat, and with any one not minutely acquainted with the fictitious hand of these Shakspere forgeries it might readily pass as genuine. But an examination of the handwriting

Augustine Phillips,
William Shakespeare,
William Kempe,
William Slye,
Nicholas Tooley.

" This remarkable paper has, perhaps, never seen the light from the moment it was presented, until it was very recently disco-vered. It is seven years anterior to the date of any other au-thentic record, which contains the name of our great dramatist, and it may warrant various conjectures as to the rank he held in the company in 1596, as a poet and as a player."—COLLIER, *Annals of the Stage*, vol. i. p. 207.

I endeavoured but unsuccessfully to see this " petition of the inhabitants," mentioned at the commencement of the above quo-tation. In reply to an official request for the production of the document, Charles Lechmere, Esq., Assistant Keeper of State Papers, writes, " I have referred to the Calendar of 1596, but I do not find any entry of the Petition from the inhabitants of the Blackfriars." Thus of these two documents, *one is an undoubted forgery—the very existence of the other seems problematical!*—[H.]

generally, the forms of some of the letters in
particular, and the spurious appearance of the
ink, led me to the belief not only that the paper
was not authentic, but that it had been executed
by the same hand as the fictitious documents
already discussed. This conviction I made known
to the Right Hon. the Master of the Rolls, who
was good enough to direct an official inquiry into
the authenticity of the document.

In accordance with this direction, on the 30th
of January, Sir Francis Palgrave, Deputy Keeper
of Public Records, T. Duffus Hardy, Esq., Assistant Keeper of Public Records, and Professor
Brewer, Reader at the Rolls, met Sir Frederic
Madden and myself for the purpose of investigation, and after a minute and careful examination
*the following unanimous decision was arrived at as
to the fact of its undoubtedly spurious character.*

" We, the undersigned, at the desire of the
Master of the Rolls, have carefully examined the
document hereunto annexed, purporting to be a
petition to the Lords of Her Majesty's Privy
Council, from Thomas Pope, Richard Burbadge,
John Hemings, Augustine Phillips, William
Shakespeare, William Kempe, William Slye,
Nicholas Tooley, and others, in answer to a
petition from the Inhabitants of the Liberty of

the Blackfriars ; and we are of opinion, that the
document in question is spurious.

"30th January, 1860.

> "FRA. PALGRAVE, K.H., Deputy-Keeper
> of H. M. Public Records.
> "FREDERIC MADDEN, K.H., Keeper of
> the MSS., British Museum.
> "J. S. BREWER, M.A., Reader at the Rolls.
> "T. DUFFUS HARDY, Assistant-Keeper of
> Records.
> "N. E. S. A. HAMILTON, Assistant, Dep : of
> MSS., British Museum."

"I direct this paper to be appended to the
undated document now last in the Bundle, marked
222, Eliz. 1596.

"2 February, 1860.

> "JOHN ROMILLY, Master of the Rolls."

So far, then, as relates to this document, the
question must be considered as set at rest :
and it is almost unnecessary to point out the
weight of the decision, not alone in regard to
this *condemned forgery*, but in respect of its
bearing upon the other writings here treated of.
Before a new edition of Shakspere is issued, or a
new life of Shakspere written, it will be necessary that the whole of the hitherto supposed
basis of the Poet's history should be rigorously
examined, and no effort spared to discover the per-

petrator of that treason against the Majesty of English literature, which it has been my object to denounce.

I here bring this list of fabrications to a close. It exhausts neither the whole of the documents which actual examination convinces me are fictitious, nor yet of those which I have only reason to suspect. But before concluding I wish to offer an observation respecting a volume in the possession of Mr. Collier, to which he has frequently drawn the attention of the public, but the authenticity of which has never, I believe, been sufficiently inquired into. I allude to a manuscript volume of Ballads, stated by its owner to have been written about the time of the Protectorate, and from which he has at various times published extracts. The most noticeable of these, which I have seen, is a ballad entitled " The Inchanted Island," the plot of which bears some resemblance to *The Tempest*; and which was published by Mr. Collier in a letter to the Rev. Joseph Hunter, in the year 1839. Far am I from hinting that Mr. Collier has any unreadiness to submit it to the most searching scrutiny. It is, indeed, through a fac-simile furnished by that gentleman to Mr. Halliwell, that I am enabled to form any opinion on the subject. But no one, I think, experienced in ancient handwritings can

look at that fac-simile,* without feeling the
gravest doubts in regard to its authenticity, which
the intrinsic character of the verses themselves by
no means serves to allay. Mr. Collier would
certainly be doing good service to the cause of
truth and literature, by bringing the volume in
question before a competent tribunal; while at
the same time he might satisfy literary curiosity,
by producing a remarkable document in connection with the history of Shakspere, various particulars in regard to which were minutely stated by
him in a letter to the Athenæum Dec. 6th, 1856,†

---

* Published by Mr. Halliwell in the first volume of his *Folio*
Shakspere, p. 312.

† " SHAKESPEARE AND HIS " RICHARD THE SECOND."

" Maidenhead, Dec. 3.

"I am afraid that I shall still further exasperate my Shake-
spearian adversaries (I wish I could say with Henry the Sixth,
' Let me embrace these sour adversaries ') when I inform your
readers that I have recently found another document, very
curiously and importantly illustrating what Coleridge used to
call 'Shakespeare's greatest historical play '—' Richard the
Second.'

" All authorities mention that shortly before the ' insurrection'
of the Earls of Essex, Southampton, &c.,—early in 1601—Sir
Gilly Merrick, Cuff, and some others of their friends, negotiated
with the Company of Actors usually playing at the Blackfriars
and Globe Theatres, in order to procure the representation of
' Richard the Second ' on the evening anterior to the rising. It
was this circumstance which made Queen Elizabeth afterwards
say to Lambard, when he presented to her his Pandects of
Records in the Tower, ' I am Richard the Second ; know you

in which he places its discovery on record, (although he does not mention *where* he found it,) but which I believe he has never yet published, and which, so far as I am aware, no one has yet seen.

---

not that?' Certain it is, that a tragedy entitled 'Richard the Second' was acted by the players of the Lord Chamberlain, of whom Shakespeare was one, on Saturday, the 7th of February, the evening before the defeat of the insane enterprise headed by the disappointed and irritated Earl of Essex. It had been the intention of the company to have acted some other more popular play on that night; but friends of the Earl of Essex had an interview with some of the leaders of the association; and at the instance of those friends the tragedy of 'Richard the Second,' (then considered 'an old play' and not likely to be attractive,) was substituted. To compensate the actors for their trouble, and for the probable loss they should sustain by the revival of an old drama, the exhibition of which, it was supposed, would advance the purposes of the insurgents, Sir Gilly Merrick and others, as was sworn upon their trial, agreed to give the performers 40s. beyond the money that might be taken at the doors.

"The document I have recovered is the account given by Augustine Phillipps, 'Servant unto the Lord Chamberlain, and one of his Players,' of what passed at the interview between the friends of the Earl of Essex and the members of the company, when the former consented to pay, and the latter to accept, 40s. on condition that they should substitute 'Richard the Second' for the play it had been their intention to perform on Saturday, the 7th of February, 1601. The date of the paper is the '18th of February, 1600;' but at that time the new year did not commence until the 26th of March, so that the '18th of February, 1600,' was, in fact, the 18th of February, 1601.

"It appears that, on the failure of the 'insurrection,' certain persons were appointed by the Crown to take the preliminary

P

I think the above is sufficient to satisfy the
reader that a series of skilful forgeries has
been practised at some late period, and apparently by some one person, on the literary

---

examinations of the different witnesses against the offenders,
and as Shakespeare was still an actor among the Lord Chamberlain's servants, as well as an author solely employed by them,
it might have happened that he would be the witness, or one of
the witnesses, to prove the agreement. We do not even know
that he was present when it was entered into ; for Phillipps tells
us that the friends of the Earl of Essex—viz., Sir Charles Pryce,
Jostlyne Pryce, and the Lord Monteagle (he does not mention
Merrick nor Cuff)—' spake with *some of the Players* in the presence of this examinant,'—but he does not give the names of the
other players, and it is very possible that Phillipps was the sole
witness to the fact on the arraignment and trial of the prisoners.
He distinctly gives the title of the play, calling it ' The Deposing
and killing King Richard the Second,' but he does not inform
us what newer and more attractive drama it was to displace, at
the instance of the two Pryces and Lord Monteagle.

" This examination is signed by Augustine Phillipps in his own
firm hand, and with both his names at length, and not merely
' A. Phillips,' as it appears at the close of his will, dated the
4th of May, 1605, and proved by his widow on the 13th of the
same month. He survived his examination, therefore, only
about four years, and died at his country residence at Mortlake.
(' Memoirs of the Actors in Shakespeare's Plays,' 8vo. 1846,
p. 83.)

" His prominence in the company in the spring of 1601, no
doubt, led to the selection of him as the person chiefly to be
negotiated with by the Pryces and Lord Monteagle, and afterwards as the witness in Court to the agreement for the representation of ' Richard the Second ' His name comes third in
the list of actors prefixed to the folio of Shakespeare's Works in

world.   Corrections of Shakspere's text, pretend-
ing to be of the seventeenth, have been proved
to be of the nineteenth century.   Documents
professedly original, relating important facts
concerning him, have been shown to have no
older or more venerable date than this or the
last generation.   I cannot disguise from myself
or my readers, that these discoveries are far
from rejoicing me.   On the contrary they seem
more suited to give a feeling of sadness.   How
far has the subtle poison, of which I have by
accident succeeded in tracking a few traces,
circulated "unknown to men" throughout the
body of our literature.   Many of the records of
the past, on which we are wont to rely, exist
only in print, and any test of their truth

1632, being only postponed to those of Heminge, the acknow-
ledged head of the association, and of Burbadge, the great
tragedian.

"The title and the whole body of this interesting document is
in the not-easily-legible handwriting of Lord Chief Justice
Popham, and it is counter-signed by him, Mr. Justice Anderson,
and Edw. Fenner, who was, I believe, at that date one of the
Queen's Serjeants. It may be recollected that Popham was one
of the Judges who went with Sir Thomas Egerton, then Keeper
of the Great Seal, to Essex House, in order, if possible, to
reason with the Earl upon the madness as well as treasonable-
ness of his proceedings."
                                    "J. PAYNE COLLIER."

beyond the doubtful one of internal evidence cannot now be brought to bear. What if "Old Correctors" were abroad then, and prudently destroyed the means of discovering their *youth!* In any case, without pushing suspicion beyond the soberest limits, the sight of successful deception is painful and unsettling. A distressing habit of doubt is apt to fasten on the mind, and a sense of helpless insecurity to overpower all other feelings.

But the history of past or present literary forgeries, does not warrant any excessive scepticism. The skill, dishonesty and knowledge, requisite for their successful perpetration, do not often meet in one individual; neither are the commercial advantages sufficiently tempting to call forth many or frequent attempts.

We cannot always penetrate the motives of crime, nor, indeed, is it always necessary that we should do this; but the good practical moral derivable from the present case, is, that greater caution in the reception of new discoveries should be practised than has been usual of late; and that no amount of incompetent laudation, however sincere or boisterous, can guarantee to the public the authenticity of recently announced Manuscript Documents.

APPENDIX I.

THE BRIDGEWATER SHAKSPERE FORGERIES.

In the Library at Bridgewater House, is a large folio containing six documents. These are all forgeries, excepting the 4th, which is genuine, and is headed, " The opinions of the two Chief Justices of either bench concerning the jurisdiccōn authoritie and liberties claymed by the Cittizens of London within the precincte of the late dissolved howses of the white and black Fryers of London delivered the xxvijth of Januarie, 1579."

A fac-simile of the fifth document in the series, executed by Mr. Netherclift, will be found at p. 83. The resemblance between the character and forms of the letters in this document and in the marginal corrections in the Duke of Devonshire's " folio," is very striking.

The text shows the exact reading of the Bridgewater MSS. Numerous verbal and literal inaccuracies exist in the professedly *verbatim et litteratim copies* printed by Mr. Collier in his *New Facts*, 1835.

No. I.

For avoiding of the playhouse in the Blacke Friers.

Impr. Richard Burbidge owith the Fee, and is alsoe a
sharer therein. His interest he rateth at the grosse
summe of 1000 li for the Fee, and for his foure
Shares the summe of 933 li 6s 8d

1933 li 6s 8d

Item Laz Fletcher owith three shares w[ch] he rateth at 700 li,
that is at 7 years purchase for eche share, or
33 li 6s 8d one yeare with an other.

700 li

Item W. Shakspeare asketh for the Wardrobe and pro-
perties of the same playhouse 500 li, and for his 4
shares, the same as his fellowes Burbidge and
Fletcher, viz. 933 li 6s 8d.

1433 li 6s 8d

Item Heminges and Condell eche 2 shares   933 li 6s 8d
Item Joseph Taylor one share and an halfe   350 li
Item Lowing one share and an halfe   350 li
Item Foure more playeres with one halfe share vnto eche of
them   466 li 13s 4d

Sum^a totalis   6166 13 4

Moreover, the hired men of the companie demaund some
recompence for their greate losse, and the Widowes and
Orphanes of players, who are paide by the sharers at
divers rates and proporcōns, soe as in the whole it will coste
the Lo. Mayor and Citizens at the least 7000 li.

No II.

*To the Right honorable Sir Thomas Egerton, Knight,
Lord Keeper of the great Seale of England.*

I will not indeavour, Right honorable, to thanke you in
wordes for this new great and vnlookt for favor showne vnto
me, whereby I am bound to you for ever, and hope one day
with true harte and simple skill to prove that I am not
vnmindfull.

Most earnestly doe I wishe I could praise as your
Honour has knowne to deserue, for then should I, like
my maister Spencer, whose memorie your Honor cherish-
eth, leave behinde me some worthie worke, to be treasured
by posteritie; What my pore muse could performe in
haste is here set downe, and though it be farre below what
other poets and better pennes have written it commeth from
a gratefull harte and therefore maye be accepted. I shall
now be able to liue free from those cares and troubles that
hetherto haue been my continuall and wearisome companions. But a little time is paste since I was called vpon to
thanke yor honor for my brothers advancement and nowe I
thanke you for my owne wch double kindnes will alwaies receive double gratefullnes at both our handes.

I cannot but knowe that I am lesse deseruing then some
that sued by other of the nobilitie vnto her Matie for this
roome, if M. Drayton my good friend had bene chosen I
should not have murmured for sure I am he wold have filled
it most excellentlie ; but it seemeth to myne humble iudge-
ment that one which is the authour of playes now daylie
presented on the publick stages of London and the possessor
of no small gaines, and moreover himself an actor in the

kinges companie of Commedias, could not with reason pre-
tend to be m^r of the Queenes Maties Reuelles for asmuchas
he wold sometimes be asked to approue and allowe of his
owne writinge.   Therfore he and more of like qualitie can
not iustly be disappointed because through yor Honors gracious interposition the chance was haply myne.   I owe this
and all else to yor Honors and if euer I haue time and
abilitie to finishe anie noble vndertaking as god graunt one
daye I shall, the worke will rather be yor Honors then
myne.   God maketh a poet but his creation wold be in
vaine if patrones did not make him to liue.   Yo^r Honor hath
ever showne yor selfe the friend of desert, and pitty it were
if this should be the first exception to the rule.   It shall not
be whiles my poore witt and strength doe remaine to me,
though the verses wch I nowe sende be indeede noe proofe of
myne abilitie I onely intreat yor Honor to accept the same
the rather as an earnest of my good will then as an example
of my good deede.   In all thinges I am yor Honors

Most bounden in dutie and

obseruance,

S. DANYELL.

No. III.

These are to sertifie yor right honorable Ll that her Ma^{tes} poore playeres, James Burbidge, Richard Burbidge, John Laneham, Thomas Greene, Robert Wilson, John Taylor, Anth. Wadeson, Thomas Pope, George Peele, Augustine Phillippes, Nicholas Towley, William Shakespeare, William Kempe, William Johnson, Baptiste Goodale, and Robert Armyn, being all of them sharers in the blacke Fryers playehouse, have neuer giuen cause of displeasure, in that they haue brought into their playes maters of state and Religion, vnfitt to be handled by them or to be presented before lewde spectators ; neither hath anie complainte in that kinde ever beene preferred against them or anie of them. Wherefore they truste moste humblie in yor Ll consideracõn of their former good behauiour, beinge at all tymes readie and willing to yeelde obedience to anie cõmaund whatsoever your Ll in your wisedome maye thinke in such case meete, &c.

Novr., 1589.

No. IV.—Genuine.

Q

No. V.

Right trustie and wellbeloved &c. James &c. To all
Mayors, Sheriffes, Justices of the peace &c. Whereas the
Queene our dearest wife hath for her pleasure and recreacōn
appointed her servauntes Robert Daborne &c. to prouide and
bring uppe a convenient nomber of children who shalbe
called the children of her Ma^tes revelles, Knowe yee that
We have appointed and authorized and by these presentes doe
appoint and authorize the saide Robert Daborne, Willm̄
Shakespeare, Nathaniel Field, and Edward Kirkham from
time to time to prouide and bring vpp a convenient nomber
of children, and them to instruct and exercise in the qualitie
of playing Tragedies Comedies &c. by the name of the
children of the reuelles to the Queene, within the blacke
Fryers in our Cittie of London and els where within our realme
of England. Wherefore we will and commaund you and
everie of you to permitte her said servauntes to keepe a convenient nomber of children by the name of the children of
the reuelles to the Queene, and them to exercise in the
qualitie of playing acording to our Royall pleasure. Pro-
vided allwayes that noe playes &c. shalbe by them presented,
but such playes &c. as haue receiued the aprobacōn and allow-
ance of our Maister of the Reuelles for the tyme being.

And these our lr̃es shalbe yo͏ͬ sufficient warraunt in this
behalfe. In Witnesse whereof &c. 4° die Janii. 1609.

Bl̄ Fr and globe   ⎫ All in
Wh Fr and parishe garden ⎬ & neere
Curten and fortune   ⎭ London
Hope and Swanne

Proude pouertie
Widdowes mite
Antonio kinsmen
Triumph of truth
Touchstone
Mirror of life
Grissell
Engl tragedie
False Friendes
Hate and loue
Taming of S
K. Edw. 2

Stayed.

No. VI.

My verie honored Lo. the manie good offices I haue
receiued at yor Lps handes wh^h ought to make me backward
in asking further favors onely imbouldeneth me to require
more in the same kinde. Yo^r Lp. wilbe warned howe hereafter you graunt anie sute seeing it draweth on more and
greater demaundes : this wch now presseth is to request yor
Lp. in all you can to be good to the poore players of the
blacke Fryers who call them selues by authoritie the Servantes
of his Matie and aske for the proteccōn of their most gracious
maister and Soueraigne in this the tyme of there troble. They
are threatened by the Lo. Maior and Aldermen of London
never friendly to their calling wth the distruccōn of their
meanes of liuelihood by the pulling downe of their plaie-
house wch is a priuate theatre and hath never giuen ocasion
of anger by anie disorders. These bearers are two of the
chiefe of the companie, one of them by name Richard
Burbidge who humblie sueth for yor Lps kinde helpe for
that he is a man famous as our english Roscius one who
fitteth the action to the worde and the word to the action
most admira[b]ly. By the exercise of his qualitie industry
and good behaviour he hath become possessed of the Blacke
Fryers playhouse wch hath bene imployed for playes
sithence it was builded by his Father now nere 50 yeres
agone. The other is a man no whitt lesse deseruing fauor
and my especial friende till of late an actor of good account
in the cumpanie, now a sharer in the same, and writer of

some of our best english playes wch as your Lp. knoweth
were most singulerly liked of Quene Elizabeth when the
cumpanie was called vppon to performe before her Matie at
Court at Christmas and Shrove tide.   His most gracious
Matie King James alsoe since his coming to the crowne hath
extended his Royall favour to the companie in diuers waies
and at sundrie tymes.   This other hath to name William
Shakespeare and they are both of one countie and indeede
allmost of one towne, both are right famous in their qualities
though it longeth not of yor Lo. grauitie and wisdome to
resort vnto the places where they are wont to delight the
publique eare.   Their trust and sute nowe is not to bee
molested in their waye of life whereby they maintaine
themselues and their wiues and families (being both maried
and of good reputacōn) as well as the widowes and orphanes
of some of their dead fellows.   Yo^r Lo. most bounden at
com̃.   H. S.

   Copia vera.

APPENDIX II.

*Forgeries among the Documents at Dulwich College:
with Extracts from Mr. J. P. Collier's Remarks upon
them.*

No. I.

" But there is another paper of a very similar kind,
apparently referring to the preceding, or to some other like
contest, but containing several remarkable allusions, which
Malone did not notice.   Perhaps it never met his eye, or
perhaps he reserved it for his Life of Shakespeare, and was
unwilling to forestall that production by inserting it elsewhere.   It seems to be of a later date, and it mentions not
only Tarlton, Knell, and Bentley, but Kempe, Phillips, and
Pope, while Alleyn's rival Burbage is sneered at as " Roscius
Richard," and Shakespeare introduced under the name of
Will, by which we have Thomas Heywood's authoritie (in
his " Hierarchie of the blessed Angels," 1635, p. 206) for
saying he was known among his companions.   The paper is
in verse, and runs precisely as follows :

> " Sweet Nedde, nowe wynne an other wager
> For thine old friende and Fellow stager;
> Tarlton himself thou dost excell,
> And Bentley beate, and conquer Knell,
> And nowe shall Kempe orecome aswell.

The moneys downe, the place the Hope,
Phillipes shall hide his head and Pope.
Fear not, the victorie is thyne ;
Thou still as macheles Ned shall shyne.
If Roscius Richard foames and fumes,
The globe shall have but emptie roomes;
If thou doest act; and Willes newe playe
Shall be rehearst some other daye.
Consent, then, Nedde ; doe us this grace :
Thou cannot faile in anie case ;
For in the triall, come what maye, ⸱
All sides shall brave Ned Allin saye."

Memoirs of Alleyn, p. 13, ed. J. P. Collier, 1841.

No. II.

" Malone also appears to have reserved another circum-
tance, of very considerable importance in relation to Shakespeare, for his life of the poet. To the last-quoted document,
but in a different hand and in different ink, is appended a
list of the king's players. The name of Shakespeare there
occurs second, and as it could not be written at the bottom
of the letter of the Council to the Lord Mayor, &c. prior to
the date of that letter, it proves that up to 9th April, 1604,
our great dramatist continued to be numbered among the
actors of the company. Hitherto the last trace we have had
of Shakespeare as actually on the stage, has been as one of
the performers in Ben Jonson's '*Sejanus*,' which was pro-

duced in 1603. We will insert the list as it stands at the
foot of the Council's letter to the Lord Mayor, &c.

        " Ks Comp.

Burbidge
Shakespeare
Fletcher
Phillips
Condle
Hemminges
Armyn
Slye
Cowley
Hostler
Day."

                                        Memoirs of Alleyn, p. 68.

No. III.

" The following undated note from Marston to Henslowe
may not be unfitly introduced here : it refers to a play by
Marston on the subject of Columbus, of which we hear on
no other authority. It is one of the scraps of correspondence
between Henslowe and the poets in his employ, existing at
Dulwich College, of the major part of which Malone has
given copies, but omitting the subsequent, which is certainly
one of the most interesting of the whole collection.

" Mr. Hensloe, at the rose on the Bankside.

" If you like my play of Columbus, it is verie well and you shall give me no more than twentie poundes for it, but If nott, lett mee have it by this Bearer againe, as I knowe the kinges men will freelie give mee as much for it, and the profitts of the third daye moreover.

" Soe I rest yours

" JOHN MARSTON."

Memoirs of Alleyn, p. 154.

APPENDIX. III.

THE INCHANTED ISLAND.

The following is the ballad alluded to p. 102, and printed by Mr. J. P. Collier, in " FARTHER PARTICULARS REGARD-ING SHAKESPEARE AND HIS WORKS. In a letter to the Rev. Joseph Hunter, F.S.A., from J. Payne Collier, F.S.A. London. Thomas Rodd, Great Newport Street, Long Acre, 1839."

" I will now," (says Mr. Collier) " introduce to your notice a production *in verse*, in my opinion written subsequently to *The Tempest*, and adopting all or most of its principal incidents. I once thought it possible that this ballad (for such it is) might have preceded the play, but I now am satisfied that it is a later production, and that the writer was acquainted with *The Tempest*, though he does not employ a single name found in it. My conjecture is that it was published (if published at all, of which we have no evidence but probability) during the period when the theatres were closed (viz. from about 1642 to 1660), in order, by putting the stories of discontinued dramas into easy rhyme, to give the public some species of amusement founded upon old plays, although the severity of the Puritans in those times would not allow the performance of theatrical entertainments. Hence Jordan's ballads, derived from *The Merchant of Venice*,

The Winter's Tale, Much ado about Nothing, &c. quoted in
my letter to the Rev. A. Dyce.   I also mentioned to him on
that occasion the ballad to which I am now adverting, and,
having since gone over it with him, I believe he concurs with
me in thinking that it is posterior to Shakespeare's *Tempest.*
The late Mr. Douce, who also had several opportunities of
reading it, at first hoped that it was the long-sought original
of that wonderful drama; and when I last saw him and
spoke of it, he was disposed to think that the play and the
ballad were derived from one common source; but though
the copying of particular expressions cannot be detected,
there are such strong general resemblances, that I feel as-
sured that the writer of the ballad must have known, if he
did not in part use, the play.   The initials at the end of the
MS. led me, when first I saw it, to conjecture that Robert
Greene, who died in 1592, might be the author of it, but it
is decidedly of too modern a cast and structure for him, and,
as I before observed, my conjecture is that it was written
about the period of the Protectorate.

I have never met with nor heard of any printed copy of it;
but it is inserted in the MS. volume I have had for years in
my possession, the particular contents of which may be seen
in my letter to the Rev. A. Dyce.   The ballads appear to
be of all ages during the century between the opening of the
reign of Elizabeth and the time of the Restoration.

Mr. Douce called it " one of the most beautiful ballads he
had ever read," and shook his venerable head (as was his
wont) with admiring energy and antiquarian enthusiasm at
different passages in it; but I am by no means prepared to
give it so high a character.   It is certainly vastly better,
both in style and sentiment, than any thing of the sort Jordan has written, and to whom the initials R. G. at the end

can apply, it would be vain to conjecture. Robert Gomersall was a poet of no mean eminence, about that period or a little earlier (he died in 1646); but it was not at all in the manner of any thing he has left behind him. It runs thus:—

THE INCHANTED ISLAND.

In Arragon there livde a king,
Who had a daughter sweete as Spring,
 A little playful childe.
He lovde his studie and his booke ;
The toyles of state he could not brooke,
 Of temper still and milde.

He left them to his Brother's care,
Who soone usurped the throne unware,
 And turnd his Brother forth.
The studious king Geraldo hight,
His daughter Ida, deare as sight
 To him who knew her worth.

The Brother who usurped the throne
Was by the name Benormo knowne,
 Of cruell harte and bolde.
He turned his niece and Brother forth
To wander east, west, north, or south,*
 All in the winter colde.

Long time he journeyd up and downe,
The head all bare that wore a crowne,
 And Ida in his hand,

---

* For the rhyme we should read " south or north," and for the sense it answers equally well. The transcriber was not a very accurate penman.—[C.]

Till that they reachd the broad sea side
Where marchant ships at anchor ride
          From many a distant land.

Imbarking ther, in one of these,
They were by force of windes and seas
          Driven wide for many a mile ;
Till at the last they shelter found,
The maister and his men all drownd,
          In the inchanted Isle.

Geraldo and his daughter faire,
The onelie two that landed there,
          Were savde by myracle ;
And, sooth to say, in dangerous houre
He had some more than human powre,
          As seemeth by what befell.

He brought with him a magicke booke,
Whereon his eye did oft times looke,
          That wrought him wonders great.
A magicke staffe he had alsoe,
That angrie fiendes compelld to goe
          To doe his bidding straight.

The spirites of the earth and aire,
Unseene, yet fleeting every where,
          To crosse him could not chuse.
All this by studie he had gaind
While he in Arragon remaind,
          But never thought to use.

When landed on thinchanted Isle
His little Ida's morning smile
          Made him forgett his woe :

And thus within a cavern dreare
They livde for many a yeare ifere,
  For heaven had will'd it soe.

His blacke lockes turnd all silver gray,
But ever time he wore away,
  To teach his childe intent;
And as she into beautie grew
In knowledge she advanced to [o]
  As wise as innocent.

Most lovlie was she to beholde;
Her haire was like to sunn litt golde,
  And blue as heaven her eye.
When she was in her fifteenth yeere
Her daintie forme was like the deere *
  Sportfull with majestie.

The Demons who the land had held
By might of magicke he expelld,
  Save such as he did neede;
And servaunts of the ayre he kept
To watch o'er Ida when she slept,
  Or on swift message speede.

And all this while in Arragon
Benormo raignde, who had a son
  Now growne to mans estate:
His sire in all things most unlike
Of courage tried, yet slow to strike,
  Not turning love to hate.

---

* This couplet is transposed in the MSS. with the figures 1 and
2 against the lines, to indicate the order in which they were to
be read.—[C.]

Alfonso was the Princes name,
It chancd posthaste a message came
    Just then to Arragon
From Sicilie to son and sire,
Which did their presence soone desire
To see Sicilia's son

Fast tyed in the nuptiall band
To Naples daughters lovelie hand,
    And they to go consent.
So in a galley on a day
To Sicilie they tooke their way,
    Thither to saile intent.

Geraldo by his magicke art
Knew even the hour of their depart
    For distant Sicilie :
He knew alsoe that they must passe
Neare to the isle whereon he was,
    And that revenge was nie.

He callde his spirites of the aire
Commanding them a storme prepare
    To cast them on that shore.
The gallant barke came sailing on
With silken sailes from Arragon
    And manie a guilded ore.

But gilded ore and silken saile
Might not against the storm prevaile :
    The windes blew hie aud loude.
The sailes were rent, the ores were broke
The ship was split by lightning stroke
    That burste from angrie cloude.

But such Geraldoe's powre that day
That though the ship was cast away,
    Of all the crue not one,
Not even the shipboy, then was drowned,
And old Benormo on drie ground
    Imbracde his dearest son.

About the isle they wandered long
For still some spirite led them wrong
    Till they were wearie growne ;
Then came to olde Geraldoe's cell,
Where he and lovelie Ida dwell ;
    Though seene they were not knowne.

Much marvelled they in such a place
To see an Eremit's wringled face,
    More at the maid they start :
And soone as did Alfonso see
Ida so beautifull but hee
    Felt love within his hart.

Benormo heard with griefe and shame
Geraldo call him by his name,
    His brothers voyce well knowne.
Upon his aged knees he fell,
And wept that he did ere rebell
    Against his brother's throne.

Brother, he cried, forgive my crime !
I sweare, since that u[n]happie time
    I have not tasted peace.
Returne and take againe your crowne,
Which at your feete I will lay downe,
    And soe our jarres surcease.

Never, Giraldo said, will I
Ascend that seat of soverainty ;
   But I all wrongs forgett.
I have a daughter, you a son,
And they shall raigne ore Arragon,
   And on my throne be sett.

My head is all too olde to bear
The weight of crownes and kingdomes care,
   Peace in my bookes I find.
Gold crownes beseeme not silver lockes,
Like sunbeames upon whitend rockes,
   They mocke the tranquill minde.

Benormo, worne with cares of state,
Which worldlie sorrowes aye create,
   Sawe the advice was good.
The tide of love betwixt the paire,
Alfonso young and Ida faire,
   Had suddaine reacht the flood.

A galley, too, that was sent out
From Sicilie in feare and doubt,
   As having heard the wracke,
Arrived at the inchanted Isle,
And took them all in little while
   Unto Messina backe.

But ere his leave Geraldo tooke
Of the strange isle, he burnt his booke
   And broke his magicke wand.
His arte forbid he aye forswore,
Never to deale in magicke more
   The while the earth shuld stand.

S

From that daie forth the Isle has beene
By wandering sailors never seene.
   Some say 'tis buryed deepe
Beneath the sea, which breakes and rores
Above its savage rockie shores,
   Nor ere is knowne to sleepe.

In Sicilie the paire was wed,
To Arragon there after sped,
   With fathers who them blessed.*
Alfonso rulde for many a yeare,
His people lovde him farre and neare,
   But Ida lovde him best.

                  FINIS.   R. G.

---

* In the MS it stands " blesse," but the rhyme clearly requires " blessed," no doubt an error of transcription.—[C.]

APPENDIX IV.

CORRESPONDENCE IN *THE TIMES* FROM JULY 2, TO AUGUST 1, 1859.*

LETTER I.

To the Editor of The Times.

Sir,—Perhaps amid the press and distraction of politics which are now agitating the great world, you can find room for the account of a most extraordinary deception which has been practised in the republic of letters, some details of which I now beg to lay before you.

In 1852 Mr. John Payne Collier published a volume containing numerous and important *Notes and Emendations* of the text of Shakspere, made, as he stated, on the faith of a copy of the folio edition of 1632, purchased by him of Mr. Thomas Rodd in 1849, and exhibiting a vast number of marginal corrections and alterations in a handwriting asserted by Mr. Collier to be, to the best of his belief, contemporary, or nearly so, with the date of the edition.

Such has been the effect of that publication throughout

---

* It has been thought advisable to reprint in a consecutive form the whole of the Correspondence which appeared in *The Times* on *The Shaksperian Discovery*, notwithstanding that portions of it have been already quoted in the preceding pages.

Europe that since the date of its issue the text of Shakspere has been extensively changed, and this, notwithstanding the strongest remonstrance and opposition from various quarters. I need not go over this ground, familiar as it is to all who know anything of the literary history of the last ten years.

In 1853 Mr. Collier published a second edition of his work, together with an edition of Shakspere founded on the corrected folio; and in 1856 what professed to be a complete list of all the readings.

"I have," says he, in his preface to this last work (p. lxxix.), "often gone over the thousands of marks of all kinds in its margins; but I will take this opportunity of pointing out two emendations of considerable importance, which happening not to be in the margins, and being written with very pale ink, escaped my eye until some time after the appearance of my second edition, as well as of the one-volume *Shakespeare*. For the purpose of the later portion of my present work I have recently re-examined every line and letter of the folio 1632, and I can safely assert that no other sin of omission on my part can be discovered."

These publications were accompanied by what professed to be a minute account of the appearance and history of the recently-discovered folio. It is, however, notorious. that by a considerable number of persons interested in the subject, the descriptions thus given were never deemed sufficient or satisfactory in a matter of such deep literary importance.

In common with others, I had often desired to see the volume, which meanwhile had become the property of the Duke of Devonshire. This wish has at length been gratified. Some two months ago his Grace, the present Duke, liberally placed the folio in the hands of Sir Frederic Madden,

Keeper of the MSS. in the British Museum, with the understanding that, while it should be kept by Sir Frederic Madden in the strictest custody, it might yet be examined, under proper restrictions, by any and all literary persons who were anxious to do so. I at once seized the opportunity, and determined, avoiding all Shaksperian criticism, to attempt an accurate and unbiased description of the volume from the literary point of view alone. Discoveries soon occurred, to which it seems advisable immediate publicity should be given, and which I now send you in as clear a manner as the narrow scope of a letter will permit.

The volume is bound in rough calf (probably about the middle of George II.'s reign), the water-mark of the leaves pasted inside the cover being a crown surmounting the letters " G. R." (*Georgius Rex*), and the Dutch lion within a paling, with the legend *pro patriâ ;** and there is evidence to show that the corrections, though intended to resemble a hand of the middle of the 17th century, could not have been written on the margins of the volume until after it was bound, and consequently not at the earliest, until towards the middle of the 18th.

I should enter more minutely into this feature of the case, did not the corrections themselves, when closely examined, furnish facts so precise and so startling in their character that all collateral and constructive evidence seems unnecessary and insignificant.

---

* I have recently investigated this point minutely, and am of opinion that the binding is even later than I had at first imagined. Paper of the same texture, and with the same water-mark, was in common use from 1760 to 1780. See Haldimand Correspondence, in the British Museum. I have seen a water-mark almost identical in Dutch foolscap of the present day.—[H.]

They at first sight seem to be of two kinds,—those, namely, which have been allowed to remain, and those which have been obliterated with more or less success, sometimes by erasure with a penknife or the employment of chemical agency, and sometimes by tearing and cutting away parts of the margin. The corrections thus variously obliterated are probably almost as numerous as those suffered to remain, and in importance equal to them. Whole lines, entire words, and stage directions have been attempted to be got rid of, though in many instances without success, as a glance at the various readings of a first portion of *Hamlet*, which I subjoin, will show.

Of the corrections allowed to stand, some, on a hasty glance, might, so far as the handwriting is concerned, pass as genuine, while others have been strangely tampered with, touched up, or painted over, a modern character being dexterously altered by touches of the pen into a more antique form. There is, moreover, a kind of exaggeration in the shape of the letters throughout, difficult, if not impossible, to reconcile with a belief in the genuineness of the hand; not to mention the frequent and strange juxtaposition of stiff Chancery capital letters of the form in use two centuries ago with others of a quite modern appearance : and it is well here to state that all the corrections are evidently by one hand; and that, consequently, whatever invalidates or destroys the credit of a part, must be considered equally damaging and fatal to the whole.

At times the correction first put in the margin has been obliterated, and a second emendation substituted in its stead, of which I will mention two examples which occur in *Cymbeline* (fol. 1632, p. 400, col. 1) :—

" With Oakes unshakeable and roaring Waters,"

where *Oakes* has first been made into *Cliffes*, and subsequently into *Rockes*. Again (p. 401, col. 2) :—

" Whose Roof's as low as ours: Sleepe Boyes, this gate,"
on the margin (a pencil cross having been made in the first
instance) *Sleepe* is corrected into *Sweete*, afterwards *Sweete*
has been crossed out, and *Stoope* written above.

There is scarcely a single page throughout the volume in
which these obliterations do not occur. At the time they
were effected it is possible the obliteration may have appeared
complete ; but the action of the atmosphere in the course of
some years seems in the majority of instances to have so far
negatived the chemical agency as to enable the corrections
to be readily deciphered. Examples of these accompany
this letter, and I shall be surprised if in the hands of Shaksperian critics they do not furnish a clue to the real history
of the corrector and his corrections.

I now come to the most astounding result of these investigations, in comparison with which all other facts concerning the corrected folio become insignificant. On a close
examination of the margins they are found to be covered
with an infinite number of faint pencil-marks and corrections, in obedience to which the supposed old corrector has
made his emendations. These pencil corrections have not
even the pretence of antiquity in character or spelling, but
are written in a bold hand of the present century. A remarkable instance occurs in *Richard III.* (fol. 1632, p. 181,
col. 2), where the stage direction, " with the body," is
written in pencil in a clear modern hand, while over this the
ink corrector writes in the antique and smaller character
" with the dead bodie," the word " dead " being seemingly
inserted to cover over the entire space occupied by the
larger pencil writing, and " bodie " instead of " body " to

give the requisite appearance of antiquity. Further on, in the tragedy of *Hamlet* (fol. 1632, p. 187, col. 1) :—

" And crooke the pregnant Hindges of the knee,"
" begging " occurs in pencil in the opposite margin, in the same modern hand, evidently with the intention of superseding " pregnant " in the text. The entire passage from, " Why should the poore be flatter'd ?" to " As I doe thee. Something too much of this " was afterwards struck out. The ink corrector, probably thrown off his guard by this, neglected to copy over and afterwards rub out the pencil alteration, according to his usual plan, and by this oversight we seem to obtain as clear a view of the *modus operandi* as if we had looked over the corrector's shoulder and seen the entire work in process of fabrication. I give several further instances where the modern pencil-writing can be distinctly seen underneath the old ink correction ; and I should add that in parts of the volume, page after page occurs in which commas, notes of admiration and interrogation, &c., are deleted or inserted in obedience to pencil indications of precisely the same modern character and appearance as those employed in correcting the press at the present day. *Twelfth Night* (fol. 1632, p. 258, col. 1) :—" I take these wise men, that crow so at these set kind of fooles, no better than the fooles Zanies." The corrector makes it " *to be* no better than," &c. Here the antique " to be " is written over a modern pencil " to be " still clearly legible. A few lines further down the letter *l* is added in the margin over a pencil *l*.

In *Hamlet* (fol. 1632, p. 278, col. 1) :—

" Oh, most pernicious woman !"
is made into—

" Oh, most pernicious and perfidious woman !'

But here, again, the "perfidious" of the corrector can be seen to be above a pencil "perfidious" written in a perfectly modern hand.

In *Hamlet* (fol. 1632, p. 276, col. 2) the line

"Looke too't, I charge you; come your way,"

has been altered by the corrector into

"Looke too't, I charge you; *so now* come your way"

in the inner margin. The words "so now," in faint pencil and in a modern hand, on the outer margin, are distinctly visible. Immediately below this, and before

"*Enter* Hamlet, Horatio, Marcellus,"

the corrector has inserted "Sc. 4." This would seem to have been done in obedience to a pencil "IV." in the margin.

In *King John* (fol. 1632, p. 6, col. 2),

"Austria and France shoot in each other's mouth.

The corrector adds, as a direction, at this line "aside;" the same word "aside" occurs likewise in pencil in a modern hand on the outer margin.

I have thus endeavoured to give, in a dispassionate manner, and as clearly as the limited scope of a letter will admit, the grounds upon which I conceive it positively established that the emendations, as they are called, of this folio copy of *Shakspere*, have been made in the margins within the present century. What further deductions may be drawn from the large mass of hitherto unpublished alterations which the folio contains I leave others to determine. They may or may not be the means of identifying particular persons or particular dates, but in the main issue are comparatively unimportant.

T

While I am personally responsible for the conclusions I have been driven to by the discovery of the above-mentioned facts, the accuracy of the facts themselves and the fidelity of my statement of them have been carefully and scrupulously examined by men having greater ability and experience in such matters than I can lay claim to. Moreover, these are points which may be tested by any persons interested in the subject, and who will be at the pains of verifying for themselves the truth of what I have here advanced. I have only to add that I hope shortly to lay before the public, in another form and in fuller detail, other particulars relating to this remarkable volume.

I am, &c.,

N. E. S. A. HAMILTON.

Department of MSS.,
  British Museum, June 22.

LETTER II.

To the Editor of the Times.

SIR,—I trust to your sense of justice, to say nothing of my ancient connection with your establishment (see especially the *Times* of the summer of 1819), for the insertion of this letter with as much prominence as you gave to that of Mr. Hamilton in your paper of July 2. As I live entirely in the country, and take in only a weekly publication, I did not see your paper containing that letter until an hour ago. I shall reply to it briefly and positively.

First, as to the pencillings in the corrected folio, 1632, which I accidentally discovered. I never made a single pencil-mark on the pages of the book, excepting crosses,

ticks, or lines, to direct my attention to particular emendations.* I have not seen it for four or five years, but I
remember that on the board at the end (there was no fly-
leaf there) I wrote various words, and made several notes,
which I never attempted to erase. There they probably
remain ; and if the pencilings of which Mr. Hamilton speaks,
in the body of the volume, were made by me, they may be
compared with my writing on the last board, and by that
writing I may be convicted, unless somebody, which I do
not believe, have taken the pains to imitate my hand.
What is clearly meant, though somewhat darkly expressed,
is that I am the author both of the pencillings and of the
notes in ink.

I have asserted the contrary on oath in an affidavit
sworn and filed in the Queen's Bench, on Jan. 8, 1856. I
assert the contrary now, and if any person will give me
the opportunity, I am ready to confirm it by my *vivâ voce*
testimony, and to encounter the most minute, the most
searching, and the most hostile examination.

I have shown and sworn that this very book was in the
possession of a gentleman named Parry about half a century
ago, given to him by a relation named George Gray. Mr.
Parry recognized it instantly, annotated as it is now ; and
since it came into my hands, in 1849, I have not made the
slightest addition to the notes in pencil or in ink.

Then, as to the binding. I contend that it is considerably older than the reign of George II., and that the

---

* I ought to add, that I drew pencil lines round 18 additional
fac-similes from the volume, admirably executed by Mr. Netherclift, copies of which I furnished to my friends, to enable them
the better to judge of the general mass of emendations.—[C.]

date of the fly-leaf affords no criterion as to the date when
the leather covering was put on, and for this reason, that
fly-leaves are often added at a subsequent period for the pro-
tection of the title-page, because the original ones have been
torn or destroyed. Upon my own shelves I have several
distinct proofs of this fact, but I will only mention one. It
is a copy of Samuel Daniel's *Panegyricke Congratulatory*, folio
(1603), which the poet presented to the Countess of Pem-
broke; Daniel wrote her name on the gilt vellum cover,
and she put her signature on the title-page. It is likely
that Daniel also placed an inscription on the fly-leaf, which
has disappeared, perhaps to gratify the cupidity of some
autograph collector. A comparatively modern substitute
has been inserted; it has no water-mark, but a moment's
inspection is enough to show that it was much posterior to
the time when the book was printed.

The rough calf binding of the corrected folio, 1632, I
contend is old; it is the same as Lord Ellesmere's copy of
the same edition; the fly-leaf described by Mr. Hamilton is
comparatively new; but I have all along admitted, privately
and in print, that the rough calf binding of the corrected
folio, 1632, was the second or third coat the book had worn.

In the same way, as to imperfect erasures and alterations of emendations, denoting changes of mind or better
information on the part of the maker of the old marginal
notes, I have been as distinct and emphatic as anybody, in
both the editions of my volume of *Notes and Emendations* in
1852 and 1853. Mr. Hamilton can, I think, point out
nothing that I have not anticipated.

Soon after I discovered the volume, and before I had
written more than a letter or two in the *Athenæum* upon it,
produced it before the Council of the Shakspeare Society—

at the general meeting of that body—at two or three evening assemblies of the Society of Antiquaries; and in order
that it might not escape the severest scrutiny by daylight, I
advertised that it would be left for a whole morning in the
library of that society for the inspection of anybody who
wished to examine it. I did not see Mr. Hamilton there,
but no one who inspected it discovered, or at least pointed
out, any of the pencil-marks which it seems are now visible.

I shall say nothing of the indisputable character of
many of the emendations. The Rev. Mr. Dyce has declared, in his own handwriting, that 'some of them are so
admirable that they can hardly be conjectural,' and in the
course of his recent impressions of the works of Shakspeare,
he has pronounced such as he unavoidably adopted, irre-
sistible, indubitable, infallible, &c. All this I might have
appropriated to myself; and, having burnt the corrected
folio, 1632, I might have established for myself a brighter
Shakspearian reputation than all the commentators put
together. If, therefore, I have committed a fraud, it has
been merely gratuitous. I certainly preferred a different
course, in spite of the warning given me by a friend in the
outset, that my enemies would never forgive my discovery,
and that their hostility would outlive my existence.

I am determined not to make the poor remainder of my
life miserable by further irritating contests; this is the last
word I shall ever submit to say upon the subject in print,
but if the matter be brought before a proper legal tribunal,
I shall be prepared in every way to vindicate my integrity.

May I be allowed to add a word in answer to certain
paragraphs stating that the late Duke of Devonshire gave
me a large sum for my corrected folio, 1632? It was a
free gift on my part, frankly accepted by his Grace, although

he afterwards (knowing of my family bereavements and consequent expenses) unsuccessfully endeavoured to persuade me to accept £250 for the volume. The Duke was at Chatsworth when I sent my letter to him, stating that the book was a poor return for the many essential and substantial favours I had received at his hands during a period of thirty years, and on June 20, 1853, his Grace wrote me a letter containing the following words :—

"It is impossible for me to express how much I am gratified by your present, on which I shall place great value, not only for the merits and interest that accompany it, but as a proof of your enduring friendship and approbation."

It is clear, therefore, that if without motive I imposed upon the public, I did not without conscience victimise the man to whom I was already so deeply indebted.

I am, &c.,   J. PAYNE COLLIER.

Riverside, Maidenhead, July 5.

LETTER III.

To the Editor of the Times.

SIR,—As it has been suggested to me that I should put on record some observations regarding the singular Shaksperian discovery recently made in the MSS. department here, I hope this letter will be sufficient explanation for my appearance on the scene in the discussion now going on regarding it.

There are three kinds of evidence that may be brought to bear on a literary forgery. The intrinsic literary character of the document is one of these. Another is of a palæological kind, and its value is to be estimated by the amount of experience and antiquarian erudition and skill of the critic. There is a third to which I would more particularly invite attention in this letter, and that rests on the physical scrutiny of the document, by the aids which science has placed in our hands.

There is, indeed, another direction in which such an inquiry may be pursued, and which has to deal in circumstantial evidence—such as individual handwriting, or the tracing of analogous documents into a single channel, or in other details highly interesting to the literary " detective," but not congenial to an officer of the British Museum. The officers, indeed, of a great national establishment like the Museum owe a duty to the public, and, in a certain sense occupy a judicial position in questions like this under discussion. Thus, while our object is not to trace the hand in a forgery, it is our duty to denounce the forgery itself. It is in this spirit that I have approached the subject, and it is with the physical aspects of it alone that I have to deal.

Mr. Hamilton, a gentleman at the time only slightly known to me as an officer of this establishment, informed me some days since that the Duke of Devonshire had intrusted the far-famed Collier's *Shakspere* to the hands of my colleague, Sir Frederic Madden, for the inspection of literary men ; and Mr. Hamilton further informed me of the doubts which, after a careful scrutiny of the volume, had arisen in his mind regarding its genuineness. His reasons for these doubts he has since made public by his letter in *The Times*. On his mentioning the existence of a vast number of partially obliterated pencil-marks, which seemed anticipatory of the ink " emendations " of " the old commentator," I suggested the use of an instrument which has already done

good service in an analogous case (that of the Simonides'
Uranius)—the microscope. This simple test of the character
of these emendations I brought to bear on them, and with
the following results. Firstly, as to any question that
might be raised concerning the presence of the pencil-marks,
asserted to be so plentifully distributed down the margin,
the answer is, they are there. The microscope reveals the
particles of plumbago in the hollows of the paper, and in no
case that I have yet examined does it fail to bring this fact
forward into incontrovertible reality. Secondly, the ink
presents a rather singular aspect under the microscope. Its
appearance in many cases on, rather than in, the paper,
suggested the idea of its being a water-colour paint rather
than an ink ; it has a remarkable lustre, and the distribution
of particles of colouring matter in it seem unlike that in
inks, ancient or modern, that I have yet examined.

This view is somewhat confirmed by a taste, unlike the
styptic taste of ordinary inks, which it imparts to the tongue,
and by its substance evidently yielding to the action of
damp. But on this point, as on another, to which attention
will presently be drawn, it was not possible to arrive at a
satisfactory conclusion in the absence of the Duke of Devonshire's permission to make a few experiments on the volume.

His Grace visited the Museum yesterday, and was good
enough to give me his consent to this. The result has been
that the suspicions previously entertained regarding the ink
were confirmed.

It proves to be a paint removable, with the exception of a
slight stain, by mere water, while, on the other hand, its
colouring matter resists the action of chymical agents which
rapidly change inks, ancient or modern, whose colour is due
to iron. In some places, indeed, this paint seems to have

become mixed, accidentally or otherwise, with ordinary ink, but its prevailing character is that of a paint formed perhaps of sepia, or of sepia mixed with a little Indian ink. This, however, is of secondary importance in comparison with the other point which has been alluded to. This point involves, indeed, the most important question that has arisen, and concerns the relative dates of the modern-looking pencil-marks and the old emendations of the text which are in ink. The pencil-marks are of different kinds. Some are d's, indicative of the deletion of stops or letters in the text, and to which alterations in ink, I believe, invariably respond. Others, again, belong to the various modes at present in use to indicate corrigenda for the press. Some may, perhaps, be the "crosses, ticks, or lines," which Mr. Collier introduced himself. But there are others again in which whole syllables or words in pencil are not so effectually rubbed out as not to be still traceable and legible, and even the character of the handwriting discernible, while in near neighbourhood to them the same syllable or word is repeated in the paint-like ink before described. The pencil is in a modern-looking hand, the ink in a quaint, antique-looking writing. In several cases, however, the ink word and the pencil word occupy the same ground in the margin, and are one over the other. The question that arises in these cases, of whether these two writings are both ancient or both modern, or one ancient and the other modern, is a question for the antiquary or palæographist. The question of whether the pencil is antecedent or subsequent to the ink, is resolvable into a physical inquiry as to whether the ink overlies the pencil, or the pencil is superposed upon the ink. The answer to this question is as follows :—

I have nowhere been able to detect the pencil-mark clearly overlying the ink, though in several places the pencil

U

stops abruptly at the ink, and in some seems to be just traceable through its translucent substance, while lacking there the general metallic lustre of the plumbago. But the question is set at rest by the removal by water of the ink, in instances where the ink and the pencil intersected each other. The first case I chose for this was a *u* in *Richard II.*, p. 36. A pencil tick crossed the *u*, intersecting each limb of that letter. The pencil was barely visible through the first stroke, and not at all visible under the second stroke of the *u*. On damping off the ink in the first stroke, however, the pencil-mark became much plainer than before, and even when as much of the ink-stain as possible was removed, the pencil still runs through the ink line in unbroken, even continuity. Had the pencil been superposed on the ink, it must have lain superficially upon its lustrous surface and have been removed in the washing. We must, I think, be led by this to the inference that the pencil underlies the ink—that is to say, was antecedent to it in its date; while, also, it is evident that the " old commentator " had done his best to rub out the pencil writing before he introduced its ink substitute.

Now, it is clear that evidence of this kind cannot by itself establish a forgery. It is on palæographical grounds alone that the modern character of the pencillings can be established; but, this point once determined in the affirmative, the result of the physical inquiry certainly will be to make this " old commentator " far less venerable.

I am, Sir, your obedient servant,

NEVIL STORY MASKELYNE,

Keeper of the Mineral Department.

Mineral Department,
British Museum, July 13.

To the Editor of the Times.

SIR,—When bringing before your notice, in my letter of the 22nd of June, various reasons which induced me to question the genuineness of Mr. Collier's annotated folio of 1632, I stated that my main ground, for repudiating the authenticity of the supposed ancient corrections, lay in the fact that, while they were made in an antique handwriting and spelling, having some resemblance to that used in the 17th century, they could be shown in numerous instances to be written sometimes by the side of and sometimes actually upon the same space as similar pencil emendations made on the margins in a modern hand, in a modern spelling, and to the best of my belief within the present century. Since writing that letter to you I have deemed it my duty to go over a further portion of the volume with the greatest possible scrupulousness. The results at which I arrive are the same; and I am now prepared to say that what I then considered highly probable as to the spurious nature of the corrections, is now, to my mind, absolutely certain. That in the great majority of instances the crosses, ticks, and the literal and verbal emendations occurring in pencil throughout the volume are intended to direct the ink corrections, is evident to every one who has examined the book with reference to that point. The instances in which I miss almost entirely the presence of pencil indications are where a whole line of text or a stage direction is inserted; but here, from the obvious difficulty of rubbing out entire sentences, the annotator would naturally have avoided making his emendations first in pencil. In several cases, where whole words are written in pencil, it is a suspicious circumstance that the pencil spelling is modern, while that of the ink is old—for instance, "body," "offals," in pencil; "bodie," "offalls," in ink. The pencil-marks, which occur by hundreds, though naturally faint from having been partially rubbed out, are, nevertheless, visible and distinct; in some cases, indeed, have not been rubbed out at all. It is impossible to convey to the reader, without the aid of *fac-similes*, an exact idea of their perfectly current and modern form. I can only state that they appear to me clearly of this century, and, in fact, as if written but yesterday. Yet, that they were placed on the margins previously to the antique-looking ink corrections, which in many instances they actually underlie, has been proved by Mr. Maskelyne, keeper of the mineral department. Whatever, therefore, be the intrinsic worth we may attach to such of the suggestions as are not found elsewhere, they must strictly be regarded as coming before us in a hand not of the 17th, but of the 19th century, and judged of from that point of view alone.

In regard to the ink corrections it should be stated that, although at first sight they bear considerable resemblance to the set Chancery hand of the 17th century, yet on a minute examination they will not readily support that character, their genuineness on palæographic grounds alone being very suspicious, not to say impossible; while the spurious character of the ink itself has been proved by Mr. Maskelyne.

One point alone remained, which it seemed absolutely impossible to reconcile with the belief that the corrections were of quite recent date; namely, the statement made in various publications by Mr. Collier, and also in his letter published in *The Times* on the 5th of the present month, that the volume and its corrections had been identified by its former possessor, Mr. Parry, as being in the same state as when in his hands half a century ago. " I have shown and sworn," * Mr. Collier says, in the letter above referred to, " that this very book was in the possession of a gentleman named Parry about half a century ago, given to him by a relation named George Gray. Mr. Parry recognised it instantly, annotated as it is now." Here, apparently, was positive evidence. But not so. A common friend of Mr. Collier and Mr. Parry, anxious to clear away the aspersions cast upon the folio, and to offer to the world a guarantee that the volume was in the same condition as to corrections, at the present moment, as when first in Mr. Parry's hands, requested that gentleman to go to the Museum and identify the volume. With this object Mr. Parry called upon Sir Frederic Madden on the morning of to-day (July 13th). His surprise was hardly less than our own to find, on the volume being shown to him, that it differed in edition, in binding, in corrections—in fact, in every particular in which a book can differ—from the folio *Shakspere* formerly in his possession, and which he expected to have placed before him.

Thus has the last testimony to the authenticity of this volume failed as completely and more remarkably than any of the preceding. If any one still thinks to maintain its integrity, it must clearly be on different or rather on oppo- site evidence to that hitherto adduced in its behalf. I forbear to comment on facts which I cannot elucidate, but

---

* On referring to Mr. Collier's affidavit made in the Queen's Bench, January 8, 1856, I do not find that he actually swore to the identification of the volume by Mr. Parry.—H.

the world will no doubt anxiously wish for explanations which the interests of literature seem imperatively to demand.

As it has been objected that my opinion in regard to the modern character of the cover and binding is incorrect, I think it right to state that I have since made inquiries on the subject, both of men intimately acquainted with large libraries, and also of practical bookbinders. The reply I obtain from both entirely confirms my original statement. Rough sheep (not rough calf), such as this volume is bound in, is of late introduction, hardly reaching back to the first Georges, while the brown Bristol millboard which stiffens the cover is still more recent, a gray and softer kind of board having been employed till within the last hundred years.*

Regarding the main question, I have nothing further to add; but before concluding I deem it my duty to notice two points in Mr. Collier's letter. In the first place, he says, " I never made a single pencil-mark on the pages of the book, excepting crosses, ticks, or lines to direct my attention to particular emendations," whereas sentences and notes occur in Mr. Collier's handwriting throughout the margins. I build nothing on this beyond the reflection that a gentleman may in perfect good faith make statements contrary to fact, and which he would probably not have put forth if his recollection were more exact.

The second is the following assertion made by Mr. Collier in regard to my letter. He says,—" What is clearly meant, though somewhat darkly expressed, is that I am the author both of the pencillings and of the notes in ink."

---

* See note p. 133.

Now, I wish to say that I never "clearly meant" or "darkly expressed" anything of the kind. My statement was that I considered a literary deception had been practised—a belief which I still maintain to be borne out by facts, and which I see no reason to modify or abandon. There I am well content to leave a subject which I entered into, not in the spirit of a controversialist, still less as a personal accuser.

I am, Sir, your obedient servant,

N. E. S. A. HAMILTON.

Department of MSS.,
British Museum, July 13.

LETTER V.

To the Editor of the Times.

Sir,—I feel most unwillingly compelled to say one other word respecting the corrected folio of Shakspeare's works in 1632, which came into my hands in 1849.

According to Mr. Hamilton's letter, inserted in your paper of the 16th inst., Mr. Parry states that the book which he owned, and which was given to him by his relative, Mr. George Gray, about 50 years ago, was an edition different from the folio of 1632, with different corrections.

I saw Mr. Parry twice upon the subject in the year 1853 —first at his house in St. John's Wood, when he told me (as he had previously told a common friend), that he had recognized the corrections instantly, from the fac-simile which accompanied the earliest edition of my *Notes and Emendations*, 8vo, 1852. Very soon afterwards, for greater satisfaction, I brought the corrected folio of 1632 from Maiden-head to London, and took it to St. John's Wood, but I failed to meet with Mr. Parry at home. I therefore paid a third visit to that gentleman, again carrying the book with me. I met him coming from his house, and I informed him that I had the corrected folio of 1632 under my arm, and that I was sorry he could not then examine it, as I wished. He replied—"If you will let me see it now, I shall be able to state at once whether it was ever my book." I therefore showed it to him on the spot, and, after looking at it in several places, he gave it back to me with these words:— "That was my book, it is the same, but it has been much ill-used since it was in my possession."

I took Mr. Parry's word without hesitation; and it certainly gave me increased faith in the emendations, to which I never applied a microscope or magnifying glass beyond my own spectacles. I was then living in the house of my brother-in-law; and, almost from day to day, I showed him such of the emendations of Shakspeare's text in the corrected folio of 1632 as seemed most striking or important.

If there be upon the volume any pencillings by me, beyond crosses, ticks, and lines, they will speak for themselves; they have escaped my recollection, and, as I stated in my former letter, I have not seen the book for several years. Perhaps the microscope used by Mr. Hamilton might discover that the plumbago of my pencil was the same as that of other marks, said to be in connection with some of the emendations.

J. PAYNE COLLIER.

Maidenhead, July 16.

LETTER VI.

To the Editor of the Times.

Sir,—I beg to forward you the following communication, which I have just received from Mr. Parry in reference to Mr. Collier's letter of the 16th inst.

I may add, that Mr. Parry states, in conversation, that his *Shakspere* was bound in smooth dark leather, with a new back, which was lettered, that there was no name of any former possessor written on the cover; and that part of the margins containing the emendations had been ploughed off by the carelessness of the binder.

On the other hand, Mr. Collier's folio is of the edition of 1632; it is bound in rough light-coloured sheep, not re-backed nor lettered at all; has on the upper cover, written in a bold recent hand, "Tho. Perkins his Booke:" and the corrections have not been injured by the binding.

I am, Sir, your obedient servant,

N. E. S. A. HAMILTON.

Department of MSS.,
   British Museum, July 29.

——————

"*July* 28, 1859.

" My dear Sir,—In reply to your application I have only to make the following statement, in which you will see that Mr. Collier's memory and mine are in question.

" In Mr. Collier's letter to *The Times*, printed July 19, 1859, he states that he was coming to call on me in 1853 with 'the corrected folio of 1632 under his arm,' and that he showed it to me on the road, and that I gave it back to

X

him with these words, ' That was my book—it is the
same; but it has been much ill-used since it was in my
possession."

" Now, I believe Mr. Collier to be utterly incapable of
making any statement which is not strictly in accordance
with his belief. I remember well meeting him, as he says,
in the road, and as I was then very lame, from having hurt
my knee by a fall, and was using sticks to assist me in
walking, he kindly did not allow me to turn back, but walked
with me in the direction I was going. I well remember
some of the conversation we had during our walk; but I
have not the slightest recollection that the volume of
Shakspere was then under his arm, or of my having asserted
that ' it was my book.'

" Previously to this interview with Mr. Collier he had
shown me the *fac-simile* which he mentions in his letter, when
I immediately said, on seeing it, that it was from my book.
I now believe that I was mistaken, and that I was too hasty
in so identifying *the volume* from a fac-simile of a part of a
page of it. At that time Mr. Collier knew that there were
several corrected folios of *Shakspere* in existence, but he
did not tell me that there were. At that time I did not
know that there was any other corrected folio in existence,
and I therefore supposed that Mr. Collier's fac-simile could
only have been taken from my book. It was not till the
14th of this month that I learnt from Sir Frederic Madden
that there are five or six corrected folios now in being, but
he (Sir Frederic) did not tell me so till he had laid on the
table Mr. Collier's corrected folio, and then he seemed surprised that I did not recognise it.

" Again I repeat, that having frequently since the 14th
of this month, when I saw Sir Frederic Madden, tried to

recollect everything about the book, I cannot remember that Mr. Collier ever showed me the book, but I well remember his showing me the fac-simile. I may be wrong, and Mr. Collier may be right.

" I have a very strong impression that *my* book was a copy of the edition of 1623, and was rather surprised when I saw Mr. Collier's ' Supplemental volume' (1853) to find that *his* book was of the edition of 1632.

" I may also add that I certainly did not tell, and could not have told Mr. Collier, that Mr. Gray ' was partial to the collection of old books,' for I believe he set no value at all on them.

" Believe me to be, my dear Sir, yours very truly,

" F. C. PARRY.

" *Mr. N. E. Hamilton,*
    British Museum, W.C."

LONDON:
PRINTED BY WILLIAM CLOWES AND SONS, STAMFORD STREET
AND CHARING CROSS.

1.

Enter Talɓ. Band. Ʇɟpoll Nim

2.

Eʁ

3.

Going

4.

God

5.

in a

6.

ſtraines, *mgo*

7.

Sing in your ſweet Lullaby,

now

9.

Wall

(aſide)

10.

Exit.
Dead bodies

11.

(apart)

onor

12.

cru

13.

Enter Ghoſt. armed as before

14.

And crooke the pregnant Hindges of the knee,
Where thrift may follow faining ɡ. Doſt thou heare?[2]

F. G. NETHERCLIFT, FAC-SIMILE LITH: 17, MILL ST., HANOVER SQ.